SOWING IDEAS TO GROWING BUSINESS

*Decoding Entrepreneurial Lessons
From The Plant World*

Amya Madan

Foreword by Padma Vibhushan,
Dr. R.A. Mashelkar, FRS

INDIA · SINGAPORE · MALAYSIA

ISBN 979-8-89322-791-8

Dedication

For my dear parents, Ashima & Vikas Madan,
and brother, Avee Madan,

Whose love, support, and optimism guide me and
inspire me every day.

"Content is my brush, creativity the colors, and communication the canvas. With passion as my guiding light, I strive to create meaningful experiences that resonate with hearts, inspire minds, and paint stories that leave an indelible mark on the world."

~ Amya Madan

FOREWORD

I vividly remember my conversation over a lunch break in our Reliance Innovation Leadership Centre. The issue was moving from an idea to impact. I said, " the idea is like a seed. But we don't eat seeds. We eat fruits, but how do we move from a seed to a fruit? We grow the tree. And seed to the tree is a long, painstaking process." That was the seed of an idea, which Amya then turned into her book (the tree) – "Sowing Ideas to Growing Business."

Amya embarked on this journey to turn that idea into reality – her book. I gave a gentle guiding hand in this journey from beginning to end. With her dedication, perseverance, and meticulous observation, she explored the world of entrepreneurship, drawing parallels between the growth of a seed into a tree and the development of an idea into a successful business. In the natural world, the growth of a tiny seed into a magnificent tree represents a remarkable journey of growth, resilience, and boundless potential.

This book encapsulates that transformative journey of an idea evolving into a thriving enterprise. Similarly, the evolution of this idea into a book is a testament to passion and perseverance backed by purpose. Amya demonstrated remarkable insight and a relentless pursuit of excellence throughout her journey by applying what she had learned from entrepreneurship to plant biology.

This book offers fascinating yet apt connections between growing plants and nurturing business. This unique seed-to-tree analogy beautifully illustrates the organic development of a business, making complex concepts accessible and relatable to a broad audience. It has been a pleasure to mentor her since the conception of this idea. Her ability to synthesize complex ideas and present them clearly and engagingly is commendable.

I am sure that "Sowing Ideas to Growing Business" will be a valuable resource for aspiring entrepreneurs, business owners, and individuals seeking to embark on their entrepreneurial journey. As her mentor, I am reminded of the boundless potential within each one of us – the ability to sow seeds of change, nurture them with care, and witness them flourish into something extraordinary.

I strongly endorse "Sowing Ideas to Growing Business" and enthusiastically recommend it, particularly to aspiring entrepreneurs, students, and professionals seeking to learn the lessons of entrepreneurship through an easy-to-understand plant analogy.

May this wonderful book find its way into the hands of countless individuals, igniting their entrepreneurial spirit and guiding them toward success.

Best wishes,

– Dr. Raghunath Mashelkar

Advance Praise of the Book

"I found the ideas and concepts in the book to be very innovative, interesting, and useful. The connections with nature were fascinating and yet so apt! This book is a must-read for all aspiring and would-be entrepreneurs/intrapreneurs as also those who have just started-up."

– Kiran Karnik, Former President, NASSCOM

"I strongly endorse "Sowing Ideas to Growing Business" and enthusiastically recommend it, particularly to aspiring entrepreneurs, students, and professionals seeking to learn the lessons of entrepreneurship through an easy-to-understand plant analogy."

– Padma Vibhushan, Dr. R.A. Mashelkar, FRS

"The book by young author Amya offers a fresh perspective on entrepreneurship. Explore captivating parallels between nature's growth process and business evolution, discovering new insights and uncharted analogies. An excellent read for those seeking to cultivate success in the fertile soil of entrepreneurship."

– Aravind Chinchure, CxO Coach and Author

"A seed is like a potent idea whose time has come..all it needs is some earth, water, and nurturing to germinate into a plant and hopefully into a tree. The journey of a start-up is exactly similar. That is why even investors contribute 'seed money' to a start-up. The following pages provide an engaging narrative penned by one of my favorite students at Symbiosis, Amya Madan, which offers unexpected analogies between plants and the entrepreneurial journey. This book is a must-read for aspiring entrepreneurs. Inspiration from nature is always powerful. Enjoy the book. Wishing Amya nothing but the very best."

– Prof. Sandeep Bhattacharya, Sr. Vice President of L & OD

"This book offers a compelling narrative that parallels the journey of an idea's transformation into innovation with the growth of a seed into a tree. Highlighting the challenges and nurturing required in entrepreneurship, this analogy prepares readers for their own business ventures. Amya skillfully brings this powerful comparison to life, making it a must-read for aspiring entrepreneurs."

– Sayantan Mukherjee, founder, The Innovators Garage

"This book ingeniously links the growth patterns of plants with business practices, highlighting the critical role of creativity. A must-read for budding entrepreneurs and B-school students ready to launch their ventures."

– Rajiv Tulpule, Creativity Professor, SIBM Pune

This book offers a unique perspective by drawing parallels between the journey of a plant and a business. Amya, with her unique lens, has converged these parallels, making it worth going through for all entrepreneurs, budding, and wannabe entrepreneurs."

– Dr. Smita Santoki, Faculty,

Trainer & Consultant for Export-Import Business

"This book nicely weaves two intertwined strands - lessons from nature and startup endeavors. Its surprising analogies, relatable anecdotes, and actionable insights make it an invaluable resource for aspiring entrepreneurs."

– Ashima Madan, founder, Ayam Multifin Services

"Its seamless exploration of the parallels between nature's growth and entrepreneurial journey kept me engaged from start to finish. A must-have for anyone seeking a new perspective toward strategic decision-making and risk management.

– Vikas Madan, Chartered Accountant - V Madan & Co

"Sowing Ideas to Growing Business" is a book that is a must-read for anyone interested in taking their enterprise from nascence to great heights. It delves into the profound comparison between the organic growth of a tree and the entrepreneurial voyage. The book is tailored for aspiring entrepreneurs, professionals, and students seeking insight into turning ideas into prosperous enterprises."

– Dr. Harpreet Bhatia, Associate Professor, Psychology

Contents

PART 3

Seed to Tree = Ideas to Impact

PREFACE

Before your mind questions, 'How can a young author in her mid-twenties offer insights into entrepreneurship?' I must confess that I may not possess the wealth of experience that many authors have. However, I strive to make up for it by bringing in a fresh perspective because I believe that experience may offer wisdom, but a new perspective breeds innovation.

As a young author, I may lack the anecdotes of seasoned veterans; however, I have tried to bring a unique lens to view the world – one unencumbered by preconceptions and boundless in its curiosity, by decoding entrepreneurial lessons from plant biology.

With over 3,00,000 business books already on the shelves and thousands more hitting the market each year, you might also wonder:

Do we really need another business book? But what if I say – this book approaches entrepreneurship from a different angle?

Why, in a world buzzing with the latest technological advancements, would anyone turn to plant biology for inspiration in starting a business?

Is this even the kind of book you'd find in the business section?

Well! In the pages that follow, I invite you to join me in exploring the known through new eyes, learning from the obvious, and connecting the dots in unexpected ways because this book lies at the intersection of two circles – PLANTS AND ENTREPRENEURSHIP.

This book takes a bold new perspective on entrepreneurship by exploring the analogy between the growth of a seed into a tree and the journey of an idea evolving into a successful business. Along the pages of this book, you'll discover a convergence of parallels between plant biology and entrepreneurial journey. You may even find some analogies you have never heard of before. They're meant to get you thinking about lots of those phenomena in plants that we observe daily but don't apply in business. Through simple examples and fresh ideas, I hope this book gives you a new perspective on connecting the dots between plants and business.

This book is the right one to read so that by the time you finish it, you can say, "Grown it to own it!- Grown an idea into a business you can call your own." Entrepreneurship is not just about running a startup; it is a mindset that can be applied in any setting, be it a business, workplace, or even a small store. Moreover, with this book, I aim to take the readers on a new journey of 'En-tree-preneurship.' You must be wondering why an extra "e" in Entrepreneurship because that extra "e" in your entrepreneurial journey is this book that you are holding, which will enable you to grow your ideas from a seed to a big tree, making you a successful "En-tree-preneur."

The journey from seed to tree is challenging, but the endeavor is rewarding because the sweet fruits await in the end. Entrepreneurship is about making an impact with your ideas, changing people's lifestyles and habits through innovation, and reaping profits—much like a farmer harvesting the fruits of his hard work. By unraveling entrepreneurial insights from plant biology and applying them to your business, you gain a nuanced understanding of the intricacies and diversity within our plant ecosystem. Simultaneously, you grasp how each step in nurturing a tree mirrors the crucial stages of establishing a startup, firmly rooting your business with the seed of an idea.

Drawing upon the insights of entrepreneurs, innovators, and business leaders who have witnessed this journey firsthand, this book explores the fundamental principles and strategies underpinning an idea's transformation into a flourishing enterprise. "Sowing Ideas to Growing Business" serves as a guide, blending the wisdom of nature with the astuteness of business acumen, enabling you to recognize the potential within your ideas and nurturing them into successful ventures. By embracing the lessons from nature and the experiences of visionary entrepreneurs, you will gain invaluable insights into navigating the ever-evolving landscape of business. So, let us embark on this expedition together, where the secrets of growth and prosperity lie hidden within the intertwined roots of nature and entrepreneurship. Prepare to be inspired, challenged, and empowered as we unravel the parallels between the growth of a seed into a tree and the development of an idea into a thriving business.

ACKNOWLEDGMENTS

This book culminates my learnings, research, and observations to decode the analogy between the plant kingdom and the startup world. It's been a journey spanning the past two years, during which I've had the privilege of sharing experiences with many amazing people who have supported and encouraged me along the way. While I can't possibly express enough gratitude in this short space, I want to extend my heartfelt thanks to everyone who has been a part of this journey. Your love, support, and patience have been invaluable, and this book wouldn't have been possible without you. Thank you for being a part of this incredible journey with me.

This book titled "Sowing Ideas to Growing Business" has been a significant personal milestone for me, not just because it's my first book but because it has been a mystical experience, primarily due to Padma Vibhushan Dr. Raghunath Mashelkar's mentorship, who has inspired and guided me throughout this journey. The seed for the writing of this book is in itself a serendipity (a happy accident, I say) that occurred during a conversation at the lunch table in our office when we discussed how the journey of a seed to a fruit-bearing tree is analogous to nurturing startups that create an impact through their ideas. So, here it is, making that idea an impactful guide, setting out to create a difference in the lives of many school students, budding entrepreneurs, B-school students, professionals, intrapreneurs, and those who have an idea in mind but are confused about where to begin.

I am grateful to Dr. Mashelkar for his invaluable guidance, unwavering support, and valuable insights while I was writing this book. His profound expertise and extensive experience have significantly helped me make this book a valuable resource for students, aspiring entrepreneurs, and business owners. I am deeply obliged to him for graciously agreeing to write a Foreword for this book despite his packed schedule.

I want to express my gratitude to my family, not only for their constant support and encouragement throughout the journey of writing this book but also for their belief in me and my endeavors, which have been a constant source of my strength. I am super grateful to my parents – Ashima and Vikas Madan, and my brother – Avee Madan, for their love and affection over the years. Mom and Dad, I want you to know how much I love you. It's no exaggeration to say that whatever I am today is because of you, and I can't thank you enough for this. Knowing that my family is behind me every step of the way has been incredibly uplifting. This book wouldn't have been possible without your support and motivation.

Words are inadequate to thank the people who graciously made time to read the early versions of my manuscript – Dr. Kiran Karnik and Amey Mashelkar, who provided me their pertinent feedback and insightful comments on the initial draft, helping me improve the overall narrative. The book benefitted immensely from your constructive feedback.

I'd like to thank Prof. Aravind Chinchure for his steadfast faith in me and encouragement to pursue my passions. Thank you for introducing me to this beautiful world of entrepreneurship and appreciating me at every milestone of my journey.

To my colleagues and the entire team at Reliance Innovation Leadership Centre – Sushil Borde, Shrikant Deo, Manmohan Singh, Omkar Patil, Kesavan Radhakrishnan, Khushboo Ghiya, and Shraddha Patare – Thank you for your encouragement during different stages of this book and for making me feel that everything is possible.

This section would be incomplete without thanking my school teachers and college professors whose lessons and teachings have left an indelible mark on my life. Adarsh Public School – the institution where I was taught to read and write for the first time. Those formative years gave me the skills and confidence to share my ideas with the world today. I remember when I was in class 8th, I got a 45-page book printed and gave it to my school Principal and teachers. Standing on the stage that day, little did I know that those early school lessons would shape me into an author today, with my very first book being published. I am immensely grateful to the APS leadership – Smt Usha Sahgal, Sh P.K. Sahgal, Mrs Pooja Malhotra, and Mr Prashant Sahgal for their invaluable contributions to my growth and development. I want to thank each of my teachers – THANK YOU! This wouldn't have been possible without your tireless efforts and commitment to educating and equipping me with the proper knowledge and skills. The lessons you taught, both inside and outside the classroom, are still fresh in my mind and are helping me achieve a little more every day.

I sincerely thank the entire Notion Press team who made this book a reality. I am grateful to my publishing consultant for my smooth onboarding and guidance at every step of the publishing process. To my publishing manager, Diya, and the entire design team for showing their commitment and perseverance in transforming the original manuscript of this book into a wonderful marvel that is now in your hands.

I'd also like to thank my friends and relatives who encouraged me constantly by asking – "How's your book going?" and kept me motivated with their kind words on days when I couldn't write satisfactorily.

And finally, my heartfelt gratitude to YOU for taking out your precious time to read this book amidst your busy schedule. It means a great deal to me. Thank you.

– Amya Madan

INTRODUCTION - MEET THE INNOVATION TREE

How can one learn entrepreneurial lessons merely by observing the growth of a seed into a tree? Within the realm of nature, an extraordinary transformation takes place, encapsulating the essence of growth, resilience, and limitless potential. It is the journey of a tiny seed evolving into a magnificent tree. This fascinating process, spanning years of patient nurturing, serves as a profound analogy for the growth of a business from the seeds of an idea. Like the seed that carries within it the potential of a majestic tree, an idea holds the promise to sprout and flourish into a thriving enterprise. Every successful business, whether a small startup or a global corporation, witnesses a remarkable journey that mirrors the organic development of a tree. It is a journey of determination, adaptation, and constant nurturing, shaping the concept into a tangible, sustainable reality. Just as a seed relies on nourishment, sunlight, and the right conditions to germinate and grow, so does an idea that needs a fertile environment to take root. This book unveils the significance of cultivating a solid foundation, fostering a culture of innovation, and embracing the power of collaboration. From the initial sparks of inspiration to the critical stages of development, it explores the crucial elements that lay the groundwork for success. However, the journey does not end with mere germination. As the sapling pushes through the soil, it encounters myriad challenges and obstacles, just as a business idea faces market forces, competition, and unforeseen hurdles. Together, let us delve into the strategies employed by entrepreneurs to navigate uncertainty, adapt to changing landscapes, and overcome adversity. Through their stories, we discover the importance of resilience, agility, and a relentless pursuit of excellence. As the young sapling matures into a robust tree, it branches out, reaching for the sky while firmly rooted in the Earth.

Similarly, a thriving business expands its reach, exploring new markets, building strong networks, and embracing innovation. We explore the strategies employed by successful entrepreneurs to scale their businesses while maintaining their core values, ensuring a sustainable and impactful growth trajectory.

THE HOLISTIC MODEL OF THE INNOVATION TREE

Let us look at the holistic model of the Innovation Tree, which recognizes that innovation is not a linear or isolated process but rather an interconnected system that requires a thoughtful and integrated approach. There are three main stages in the lifecycle of a plant. The first stage is the nascent stage, which starts from 'sowing the seeds' and is analogous to thinking of an idea for a business.

During this phase, the farmer begins by selecting viable seeds from a pool, preparing the field for germination, and finally sowing the seeds rich in specific traits required to yield a healthy crop with the best soil quality. Not only does the seed's quality or the soil's environment affect the quality of the crop, but the season in which it is sown and reaped also makes a huge difference. For a farmer, the key to success lies in being energetic, dedicated, patient, and persistent. Without these qualities, there won't be any fruits to enjoy when the season ends. During this phase, the farmer also gets help from its soilmates, 'the earthworms,' to accelerate the growth and development of the seeds sown. This phase closely resembles how individuals or entrepreneurs start their journey. They often begin with a vague idea or sometimes with many ideas when unsure which path to take. However, the right personality, backed with good support, a creative mindset, in-depth market research, and a clear understanding of the pain points of the customer, can help them sow their seed of an idea in the right demographic location during the most appropriate market trends, taking them onto an expedition of growing their business. Creativity is at the core during this phase of entrepreneurship, which catalyzes the mind of an entrepreneur to generate out-of-the-box ideas and innovative solutions for conventional problems. The seed transitions into a sapling during the second phase of its growth.

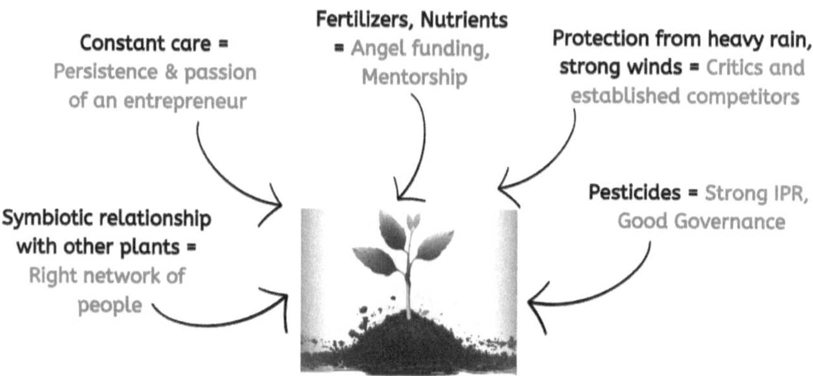

During this phase, the sapling is in its most delicate and vulnerable state, constantly handling threats from several sources, making it crucial for the farmer to provide it with utmost care. It is a gratifying period for the farmer as he sees the first tangible result of his hard work of several months in the form of a sprouted seed. During this time, the sapling needs a mix of natural nutrients, fertilizers, manures, and continuous safeguarding from strong winds and heavy rainfall. The farmers must also be careful of threats from disease and pest attacks, which could destroy the entire crop in no time. Plants also benefit from other species around them and mutually benefit each other for healthy growth, avoiding competition.

Have you ever tried growing a bonsai?

You will read through how magical it is to grow a small but strong plant in the form of a bonsai tree. For an entrepreneur, this is the stage during which they establish a prototype of their product/service, build a minimum viable product, and launch their entrepreneurial venture in the market. Like a sapling, this phase is also crucial for startups because their customers now know about their ideas. Besides customers, competitors and critics pose a challenge for entrepreneurs. Thus, it becomes essential for them to protect their entrepreneurial baby from all kinds of threats using a strong IPR and expert mentorship. The persistence of an entrepreneur also plays an integral role during this phase because they need to be patient and consistent while persuading customers, which involves marketing, sales, and operations. Plants also show unique stimulatory responses during this phase, analogous to the foresight and insight among organizations that promote an entrepreneurial mindset. Vitamin M – mentoring and money are crucial for the development of a startup, which they get through angel funding and investors. Startups should prioritize engaging in collaborative partnerships rather than feeling threatened by competition, as this approach helps establish a robust and enduring business model for sustained growth. Finally, after months and years of unwavering dedication, persistence, and hard work, there comes a stage where the seed undergoes a remarkable transformation into a substantial tree, blossoming with flowers and bearing fruits.

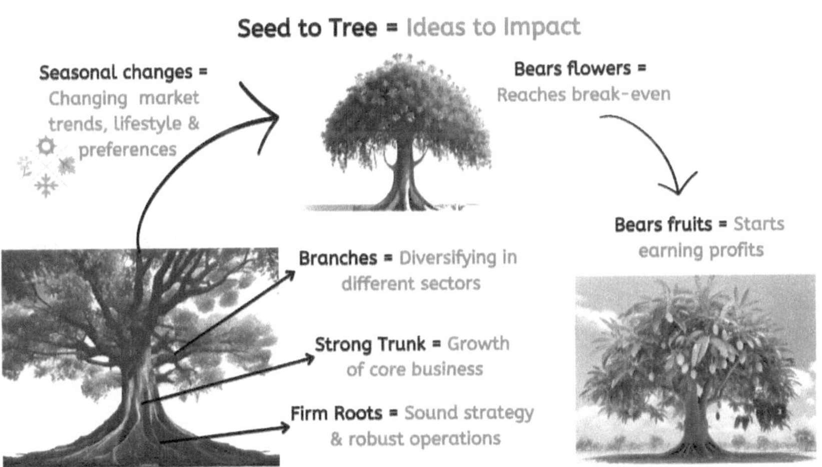

The third phase holds paramount significance for any farmer, as it is through the fruition of these fruits that they can reap the profits for the months of patience and persistence invested.

Nonetheless, this phase remains unstable for the tree, susceptible to constant impact from seasonal changes.

A seed that grew during the summer has now bloomed during the spring, so the tree has to bear the snow storms now. This tree is enormous and more diversified, having a physiological and complex anatomical structure that aids them in surviving the ravages of time. Now, the tree is all set to grow its branches, attracts bees and pollinators to its beautiful flowers, and ripens into sweet and fleshy fruits.

ISN'T IT PLANT-ASTIC? HOW WONDERFUL DOES THE TREE LOOK, GROWN FROM SUCH A TINY SEED?

That's the magic an entrepreneur creates in their lives and the lives of their target audience with their idea, leaving a lasting impact. During this phase, the entrepreneurs eventually expand their business, build a team of people, and have already gained their first few customers. They know and understand their industry better now. Hence, it's time to make some money. The tree first bears flowers, analogous to the startup reaching its break-even. Once the flower modifies into a fruit, entrepreneurs can say they have finally started earning profits, creating an impact through their innovation.

Closely looking at this journey of a seed to fruit, you will notice how similar it is to the entrepreneurial journey of an idea to an impact.

MEET THE INNOVATION TREE

"As you sow, so shall you reap." We all have grown up listening to this famous proverb. Would you like to know the meaning of this proverb from an innovative entrepreneur's perspective? This proverb is a universal truth and a way of growing in life. When you sow the seeds of a mango plant, it is impossible for a cactus plant to grow from it.

That means, for an entrepreneur as well, the type of seed (idea) sown is the genesis of their tree (startup/business). While we all look at different trees' beauty and strength, the first question still sparks is, "Where is the fruit?" Possibly, that's because we are too focused on reaching the destination; we sometimes miss out on the growth journey.

In the words of A.P.J Abdul Kalam, "Those who dare to challenge the impossible are the ones who break all the human limitations." This statement holds true for entrepreneurs ready to sow the seeds of challenging the impossible and reap a crop capable of breaking humans' limitations. The transformation of a seed into a big tree is a continuous process of growth, development, maturing, fruition, and ripening.

Let me introduce you to the innovation tree, which has found its analogy to the entrepreneur growing his business.

Say Hi!

"Aloe there!

I am a tiny apple seed. My farmer has sown me after careful inspection of the soil. He selected me from a bank of similar seeds because he found me more potent than the others. He carefully dug and prepared the soil before sowing me in it. My growth into a sapling depends on the constant support and care that my gardener provides me, along with the other ingredients such as fertilizers, nutrients, pesticides, etc. He also provides me with constant protection from strong winds and heavy rains. Few weeks back, he added earthworms in the soil to catalyze my growth so it remains well aerated. When I emerged as a sapling, he associated me with other plants as well so that I could benefit from their nutrients. After many months, I am now like a big tree. Unlike my sapling, which had a delicate stem and was vulnerable to threat, I am now much bigger and stronger. I possess firm roots, a strong trunk, and branches of various shapes and sizes.

Not only that, but over the years, I have also learned to withstand seasonal changes, thunderstorms, and heavy rainfall. Now, I have started bearing flowers that will soon turn into fruits. These fruits will benefit the farmer, who can now sell them to earn his livelihood. His patience, perseverance, and passion have transformed me from a little seed to a fruit. My journey doesn't end here. Although I have grown up strong and big, my farmer still needs to provide me with sunlight, water, and nutrients. I have helped him by dispersing my seeds across various places so that he can expand his apple orchards."

You read the story of this tiny seed that grew into a big tree with the help of the farmer who sowed it. Now, put on the entrepreneur's hat and reread this story.

"Hi, I am an idea that struck the mind of my entrepreneur while he was looking for a solution to help the people who could not find safe, healthy, and toxin-free products for their newborn babies. While he faced challenges looking for chemical-free products, my entrepreneur realized I could grow into a successful business.

In order to make me well-suited, he started aligning me with the market needs. Initially, he checked my potential and strength by pilot-testing with a few customers, and once he was satisfied with it, he checked the market quality, which would be the most appropriate way to launch his idea. It's been a few months now that my entrepreneur has been nurturing me like his baby by providing me with all that I need regarding the right mentorship, an appropriate network of people, etc. His persistence and passion have grown me into a more innovative and impactful idea now. Though I am vulnerable to criticism and threats from competitors, my entrepreneur constantly tries to make me stand out through unique value propositions. He has protected me from the external competition by providing me with a strong IPR and good governance. His creative ideas and lateral thinking helped me grow at a faster pace. Unlike the prototype, I now have a sound strategy and robust operations. I have also grown strong in my core business, so my entrepreneur has started diversifying me into different target markets such as skin care, hair care for teenagers, etc. Environmental changes occurred when the pandemic hit, startup policies wanged, and several startups entered the same industry, but my founder stood strong. He did not give up. And with his persistence, he could break even after four years of hard work, dedication, and constant care. Very soon, he will bear the fruits of his hard work by making profits and impacting the market. This is not enough; he plans to expand pan-India and globally to create an impact everywhere."

Did you notice anything similar after hearing the stories of the apple seed and the startup idea? I am sure you must have.

Further, as we move ahead with the journey of this book, we will talk in detail about all these analogies between a seed and an idea. Grabbing this book is the first sign of your passion for entrepreneurship. The first step is enough to help you climb the ladder of success. This book will be your trailblazer to achieve that goal and create a difference. So, be ready to sow your idea to grow your business.

PART 1

SOWING SEEDS = SEEDING IDEAS

1.

NASCENCE

SOWING THE SEEDS OF AN IDEA

In the words of Steven Bartlett, "A farmer doesn't plant a seed and then dig it up every few minutes to see if it has grown. So why do you as an entrepreneur keep questioning yourself, your hard work, and your decisions? Have patience, stop overthinking, and keep watering your seeds."

The seed serves as the storehouse of the plant, storing essential nutrients and food and acting as the catalyst for the development of all other plant parts, including the root system and shoot system[1].

Isn't it fascinating how a tiny seed emerges as a pivotal element in nurturing the growth of a robust and healthy tree? Indeed, it is!

A viable seed is a precursor that leads to a productive yield. Despite being the smallest component in crop production, it holds unparalleled significance, capable of dictating the success or failure of a crop in a given season. Ask a farmer about the disappointment when sown seeds fail to yield healthy trees. No, wait. Being a budding entrepreneur, ask fellow entrepreneurs whose ideas have not created an impact over the years and could not make profits.

Both farmers and entrepreneurs face identical situations, so let's dive deep into both these scenarios by considering the analogy between a seed and an idea. Before choosing which seeds to plant, a farmer assesses the condition and characteristics of their farm. It's crucial to select seeds well-suited to their specific type of soil[2]. Likewise, entrepreneurs should thoroughly study the market before deciding on an idea. This process involves conducting comprehensive primary and secondary market research and analyzing past, present, and future market trends. This approach enables them to understand their customers' needs and challenges better, helping them select the most promising idea for developing a product or service.

Like farmers selecting the most viable seeds, they examine the seed pores by compressing or testing them in water. This method helps identify the lighter seeds that float to the top and can be easily removed. Similarly, a farmer meticulously examines factors such as soil texture, soil components, and organic content. Understanding the characteristics of the soil not only enhances the yield during the harvest season but also mitigates the need for farmers to invest in expensive fertilizers and pesticides for disease control. The incorrect selection of seeds unsuitable for their farm type can result in substantial costs for the farmer, not just in terms of money but also in terms of energy and resources. Therefore, thoroughly understanding the soil's quality and type is imperative for the farmer to maximize the likelihood of achieving better yield.

As it's crucial for farmers to assess soil quality, entrepreneurs must conduct thorough market research before pursuing their ideas. This practice not only aids in comprehending customer needs and market trends but also allows for iterative thinking before investing significant sums of money and time in establishing a startup. The way a farmer selects seeds suitable for the farm, entrepreneurs should consider their target audience's geographical, political, environmental, demographic, and psychological attributes. This comprehensive understanding can help decide whether to proceed with an idea because the success of any startup hinges on having in-depth knowledge about its customers and competitors. Market research is essential for gathering information that enhances awareness of how the intended audience will respond to current or potential products and services[3]. Market research serves as the testing ground for entrepreneurs as they try to understand the potential reach of their product/service and the anticipated revenue. Market analysis necessitates a thorough market segmentation as well. Drawing a parallel to the farmer's approach, based on the size of his land, he determines the number of seeds to spread and the methods for spreading them. He ultimately selects only those seeds that align well with his soil type.

Similarly, entrepreneurs calculate the potential revenue by selecting ideas that resonate with their target market. To achieve this, entrepreneurs can employ either a top-down approach or a bottom-up approach to ascertain the size of their Serviceable Obtainable Market (SOM). The Serviceable Obtainable Market (SOM) is like a slice of pie—it's the portion of sales in a specific product area that a company can realistically grab. In simpler terms, it's like figuring out how much market share a company can get for its product in reality.

Applying the top-down market sizing approach empowers entrepreneurs to get hold of the current market as a whole, single entity. They initially view potential customers and revenue on a broad scale, gradually narrowing their focus to a segment that can be realistically targeted. This process provides a comprehensive understanding of the Serviceable Obtainable Market (SOM). For example, consider a startup offering a payment management system for ice cream parlors. Applying the top-down approach involves calculating the total number of ice cream parlors nationwide and refining the target to specific demographics with a concentration of parlors.

Further refinement occurs by tracking parlors with sufficient customer traffic to validate the payment system. The final segmentation involves identifying parlors already using a digital payment platform, as those already using it may not adopt a new system. This meticulous process brings entrepreneurs to a realistic serviceable obtainable market.

Conversely, the bottom-up approach to market sizing takes a different trajectory. Entrepreneurs initiate the process by concentrating on the value proposition of their products or services. They build and market these offerings, gradually contemplating scaling to a larger audience. Growth subsequently materializes through exploring potential sales channels, determining optimal selling prices, and identifying how much of the current market could be effectively catered to. This method involves a strategic unfolding of the entrepreneurial journey, focusing on product development and market penetration before expanding the reach and impact to a broader audience. Thus, in this approach, the startups start small and scale up by innovating their product/ service to reach a larger audience. Though there is no specific answer to which approach is better, it may vary based on the idea and the customer segment. However, in general, if the calculations of both approaches are similar, it nearly gives an accurate estimate of your serviceable obtainable market, which can be a big decision-maker in whether to go ahead with an idea or not.

This metric provides entrepreneurs with a comprehensive understanding and a nearly accurate estimate of the realistic revenue potential for the company. It is based on factors such as the demand for their product or service, consumer interests, preferences, and the competitive landscape within the marketplace. This informed understanding of the target market is indispensable for making strategic decisions, refining product/ service offerings, and realistically estimating the company's revenue potential. The more in-depth market research an entrepreneur does, the better they are positioned to sow the seeds of their ideas and nurture them into thriving ventures that resonate with their target audience.

QUALITIES OF A GOOD IDEA VS THE MOST VIABLE SEEDS

Selecting the most viable seeds for the crop is an integral step for the farmer as it determines their productivity.

For a farmer, the most viable seed is the one that is high in genetic purity, possesses good size, shape, and color, has high physical soundness and weight, and has 90-95% germination capacity[4].

Before selection, the seed undergoes rigorous testing based on its physical quality, genetic purity, physiological quality, and seed health. The physical quality test ensures the seed's cleanliness, verifying its freedom from dirt, debris, stones, dust, leaves, twigs, stems, flowers, fruit, or any other inert material.

Additionally, the seed should exhibit uniform size, weight, and color. Selected seeds must be free of undesirable characteristics such as shriveled, diseased, mottled, molded, discolored, damaged, and empty seeds[4]. Genetic purity is tested to ensure that the seeds resemble the mother in all aspects so that they have all the desired traits and possess the required resistance to diseases. The physiological quality of the seed is tested to ensure its liveliness (viability) and germination ability. Seed vigor, which determines the performance level of the seeds during germination, is also considered. A seed that exhibits excellent performance during sowing is categorized as a quality seed. Its classification as high, medium, or low vigor is based on its effectiveness in producing elite seedlings[4]. The farmer ensures that the selected seed is devoid of any fungal infection or insect infestation, both internally and externally. The seed's health is crucial, as any compromise in its well-being would diminish its physiological strength, consequently affecting the productivity of the crop. This meticulous testing guarantees the farmer's selection of the most viable seeds.

Like a farmer meticulously rejects bad seeds and chooses only the good ones, entrepreneurs must also choose ideas with a higher probability of success. They should avoid investing significant time, money, or resources in ideas that might ultimately turn unproductive. Transforming a bad idea into a good one often involves innovative thinking to enhance its value and impact. Good ideas aren't necessarily copies of existing concepts; they involve reinventing rather than renovating ideas. For example, AirBnb initially started with an experiment of providing a platform for strangers to find a room at a stranger's place to sleep on an air mattress along with breakfast service[5]. This idea did not turn out to be a great success. Later, they tweaked the idea and started providing professional photographers to their customers (landlords). This enabled them to make their property look much better than their competitors' properties to attract more customers. This turned their initial bad ideas into good and successful ones.

Arriving at the selection of ideas necessitates entrepreneurs to generate and brainstorm potential concepts initially. This can be achieved by utilizing various divergent idea-generation tools and techniques available to budding entrepreneurs. One such tool is **SCAMPER.**

SCAMPER was proposed by Alex Faickney Osborn in 1953 and was further developed by Bob Eberle in 1971[6]. The name SCAMPER is the acronym for (S) Substitute, (C) Combine, (A) Adapt, (M) Modify, (P) Put to another use, (E) Eliminate, and (R) Reverse.

This divergent tool of creativity provides seven different thinking approaches to finding innovative ideas and solutions. SCAMPER enables entrepreneurs to switch to the lateral thinking zone and challenges the status quo, which helps them explore new possibilities.

For example, The success story of McDonald's is a beautiful illustration of applying SCAMPER in the business world. This is how McDonald's applied SCAMPER to generate new and innovative ideas[7].

S- Substitute: Substituted existing dine-in restaurants with self-service counters

C- Combine: Combined children's toys with food by introducing Happy Meal

A- Adapt: Adapted new technology by introducing apps and touch screens for taking orders

M- Modify/Magnify/Minimize: Reduced the original large menu to a small one with only 9 items.

P- Put to another use: Not just a takeaway restaurant, McDonald's also became a place where people could throw parties and celebrate birthdays.

E- Eliminate: Eliminated dishes, plates, spoons, etc. by wrapping the food items in paper.

R- Reverse: Reversed the existing process where customers pay before eating

By applying the SCAMPER tool, McDonald's could generate several different ideas, which helped it to scale up its business globally.

Following the idea generation phase, the crucial step is choosing the most promising idea that can cultivate a successful business. Like a farmer discards undesirable seed varieties during selection, an entrepreneur must also employ a rejection principle when selecting the best idea from the pool of generated concepts. This is accomplished through the application of various convergent idea selection techniques. One notable method is the **PINC Filter.**

The PINC Filter is a convergent tool of creativity that can be used to choose whether to go forward with an idea[8]. This tool is applied separately to each idea to evaluate it, and then, finally, a decision is made to select the best idea.

P stands for Positive (Things that add value),

I stands for Interesting (Curious and interesting things that can be of value),

N stands for Negative (Things that reduce or remove value),

C stands for Concerns (Worrying things that could remove value)

Evaluating each idea based on these four parameters enables the ideator to measure the potential of each idea they have come up with against the others and thus allows them to select the most viable idea.

Great ideas are essential for the growth of a business. Globally, 95% of the total food comes from the seed[9]. Great ideas are the food for the economy of the nation. As of 16 Feb 2024, India had 113 unicorns with a total valuation of $ 350 billion, according to Inc42[10]. Just the way seeds contribute to food needs, good ideas create an impact that, in turn, contributes to the economic and financial needs of mankind.

NOT ALL VIABLE SEEDS GERMINATE- STARTUPS FAIL, TOO.

A farmer sows the seeds with much hope, vigor, and thrill. But many times, the seeds that he has sown fail to germinate[11]. Isn't it disheartening? Of course it is!

However, seeds don't fail to germinate without a cause. There must be underlying reasons, right? Potential causes include the seeds being seasonal, making it the wrong time for planting, or unfavorable temperature and climate conditions hindering germination. Moreover, the care the farmer provides to the seeds after sowing also plays a crucial role. Excessive water, for instance, can choke the seeds, leading to either death or dormancy beneath the soil. Conversely, insufficient water is detrimental to seed growth, causing them to dry up and fail to germinate. A lack of oxygen can also contribute to the failure of seeds to germinate.

Even if all these conditions are right, there are still instances when the seeds fail to germinate. This is called '**Damping off**'. This damping-off could be due to the soil quality or some microbial organisms or pests that eat up the seeds much before they sprout. But does this all stop the farmer from sowing the seeds? No, never.

A similar situation is faced by most entrepreneurs who begin establishing their idea in the market and launch their startup at an early stage. Sometimes, their ideas are great and have huge potential, but about 90% of startups fail[12]. 10% of startups fail within the first year[12]. Failure is most common for startups during years two through five, with 70% falling into this category[13].

Why?

The primary reason for startup failure, identified in 42% of cases, is misreading market demand—like seeds failing to germinate despite seemingly favorable conditions[14]. Just as the success of a seed hinges on the suitability of the soil it's planted in; entrepreneurs must thoroughly assess market conditions before launching their ideas. The second most common cause of startup failure (29% of cases) is running out of funding and personal resources[14]. If the farmer runs out of money, how will he irrigate the plants, buy fertilizers, or provide the required nutrients?

Similarly, for entrepreneurs, a shortage of funding spells doom for their startups. Factors such as entering the wrong market, insufficient research, poor partnerships, unfavorable locations, mismatched target segments, and inadequate marketing efforts can all contribute to the downfall of a startup.

Entrepreneurs should not be disheartened by obstacles or setbacks like a farmer who persistently sows seeds even if one fails to germinate. Instead, they should embrace these challenges as opportunities for growth and learning. Research conducted by Ganesaraman Kalyanasundaram (2018) states, "In an entrepreneurial ecosystem, the failure rate of startups is extremely high at 90%, and every startup that fails, becomes an orphan. This phenomenon leads to higher costs of failure for the entrepreneurs in the ecosystem. But failed startups have many lessons and guidance to offer potential entrepreneurs[15]."

The repercussions of startup failures extend beyond the entrepreneurs and their firms, potentially impacting employment and the nation's economy. Startups can face failure at any stage of their life cycle, whether during emergence, survival, stability, or accelerated growth. What warrants examination in the context of startup failures are the contributing factors. Foremost among these factors are the entrepreneurs themselves. Entrepreneurs possess inherent characteristics, including financial skills, business acumen, technical proficiency, and personality traits, which drive them to take on challenges (Gartner, 1999)[16]. In establishing a startup, entrepreneurs must navigate multiple challenges with limited resources, and the specific requirements vary depending on the stage of the firm's operation (Chorev, 2006)[17].

Failure of an idea is not the end of an entrepreneurial journey. The farmer doesn't stop sowing seeds because the crop is not good in a particular season. Instead, they become more considerate in choosing the right seeds, preparing the soil well, and adopting different agricultural methods to produce better crops. So should entrepreneurs do. If one idea fails, brainstorm and innovate another.

As an entrepreneur, always remember what Thomas Edison once said, "I have not failed. I have just found 10,000 ways that won't work."

The seeds I sowed for weeks were unseen,

What could become of it, I never dreamed,

An idea was invoked in a creative mind,

Was sown under the soil, only an entrepreneur could find.

– Amya Madan

2.

ENTREPRENEURIAL MINDSET
UNEARTHING FARMERS' TRAITS

What looks like dirt to most people is gold for farmers.

Farming for farmers is not a 9-5 job; it is a way of life for them. Just like a soldier, a farmer is also never off duty, even if it is an off-season. They may not seem to work, but they are on "standby," waiting to act whenever needed. Long before the sowing season begins, a farmer toils in the fields from dawn to dusk, meticulously preparing the soil. This laborious task involves thorough soil quality checks, as a single misjudgment can have a profound and devastating impact on the farmers and all the stakeholders linked to agriculture.

ANYONE CAN OWN A FARM, BUT NOT EVERYONE CAN BE A FARMER.

The above statement stands true for all those farmers who spend their days and nights working on the farm, driven by a relentless passion to meet humanity's basic survival needs. Despite facing challenges and setbacks, their unwavering commitment and perseverance are commendable. They exemplify exceptional creativity, demonstrating how to do the job despite limited resources. When a straightforward fix is impossible, they ingeniously devise unconventional solutions that effectively address the issue.

Farmers serve as good exemplars of "Jack of all trades." They seamlessly navigate the intricacies of operating machinery, managing finances, and excelling in marketing and selling their crops. For farmers, the absence of a solution is never an option. They are adept at finding solutions to every challenge, embodying the ethos of resilience and adaptability.

Entrepreneurs can learn essential lessons from farmers and apply them when growing their ideas into a tree. A farmer's peculiarities lead to a successful crop. Similarly, an entrepreneur's personality traits are critical to their business' success – passionate farmers who breathe farming in every pore of their being run successful farms[1].

Farming isn't a fixed job where you do the same things every year. It's more like the changing seasons that plants experience before they bloom. Farmers must keep up with new techniques and observe what people want to buy. Good farmers are constantly learning about new crops, fertilizers, ways to water their plants, etc. But what keeps them going is their passion for farming. A farm is just barren land without fruits unless a farmer puts life into it as seeds. Similarly, an idea is just a goof unless a passionate entrepreneur infuses life into it and grows it into a business. To make an idea grow, the entrepreneur also needs to grow with it.

Though farmers are not well-educated, they have a pursuit of knowledge and eagerness to learn new farming techniques. They spend much time learning about their land, selecting viable seeds, preparing the soil, and adopting new practices to ease their jobs. All this requires an urge to learn and grow. Similarly, entrepreneurs must pursue opportunities in markets where they can address significant challenges. They should possess an inherent desire to expand their horizons beyond local boundaries and venture globally. Success in scaling their business hinges on entrepreneurs continuously updating themselves on the latest technologies and evolving market trends. This dedication to staying informed and adaptable is key to achieving entrepreneurial success on a broader scale.

Do you think becoming a farmer is an easy job?

Well, I don't think so! Every day, a farmer deals with many new challenges that pop in unexpectedly. The crisis that clutches a farmer requires them to apply some quick thinking and creativity to dig into the solutions. Farmers must be courageous enough to look right into the problem's eyes and find an innovative solution. This makes a farmer different from others who follow a clear set of instructions written in a manual. The world of entrepreneurs is very similar to these farmers. They, too, have no control over the unexpected challenges and hurdles that might arise without notice. But what makes an entrepreneur successful is their presence of mind and creative problem-solving, allowing them to handle these challenges and innovate novel solutions for their business.

To a great extent, an entrepreneur determines and writes a startup's fate. Like the farmer, an entrepreneur is the "Brahma (creator)" of his idea who writes its destiny based on his competencies and personality traits. Researchers have always been curious about what makes entrepreneurs successful and keep them going. Many studies have looked into this and found that successful entrepreneurs have certain personality traits that make them stand out. A study by Abdullah F. et al. (2009) found that eight critical factors contribute to an entrepreneur's success[2]. These factors include being driven to succeed, focused on achieving goals, committed to their work, good at making decisions, able to handle risks, determined, skilled at networking, and optimistic about the future.

Lately, there has been a shift in the questions that researchers are seeking answers to. They are focused on two key questions: First, do certain traits predict if someone will become an entrepreneur? Second, do certain traits predict an entrepreneur's chances of success[3]? . Researchers use the Big 5 Factor personality traits to answer these questions and study entrepreneurs like Steve Jobs and Jeff Bezos. They're looking at traits like openness, conscientiousness, extraversion, neuroticism, and agreeableness. On the scale of openness to experience, entrepreneurs tend to score higher. This is because they need to adapt to changes in the world and solve new problems.

People with high openness can handle challenges well by creating creative solutions, business ideas, and products. Entrepreneurs are on the higher side of the conscientiousness scale as well. This was concluded by the study conducted by Collins et al. (2004), which found that individuals who pursue entrepreneurial careers are significantly higher in achievement motivation than those who pursue other careers[4]. Similarly, Stewart and Roth (2007) concluded that entrepreneurs are more achievement-oriented than managers. It is frequently hypothesized that those with high achievement motivation are drawn to environments in which success is more closely attributed to their own efforts rather than a larger institutional setting in which business success or failure is less a function of one's efforts[5]. Entrepreneurs also score higher than others on extraversion because of their requirement to network with people, sell their products, pitch their ideas, etc. Even if not born as extroverts, many entrepreneurs must develop this skill to emerge successful.

In contrast to these three traits, entrepreneurs score slightly less on the agreeableness and neuroticism scale. This is because, unlike others, they don't have to please others and require exceptional self-confidence to take on the risks of starting a venture[6].

In addition to the five personality traits, entrepreneurs need many other skills to turn their ideas into successful businesses. Recent research has been focusing on understanding these entrepreneurial traits, with a spotlight on innovativeness and self-efficacy. Entrepreneurs rely on a strong sense of self-efficacy, meaning they believe in their ability to achieve their goals. They also need a keen eye for innovation to spot new products and markets. These qualities help entrepreneurs execute their visions and drive their businesses forward.

Just like a farmer can't handle all the tasks alone in the field, an entrepreneur can't grow their business alone. They need to be good team players and leaders to become successful. While entrepreneurs typically start handling everything themselves, they can't sow the seeds of their ideas and navigate the market alone. They need a team, and to lead that team effectively, they must possess strong leadership skills and be team players themselves.

The team might consist of family members in farming, but the farmer still needs wisdom and leadership to keep everyone involved, motivated, and moving in the same direction toward success.

Similarly, entrepreneurs may form a team they didn't know before, but they still need leadership skills to unite everyone towards a common goal, vision, and mission, enhancing productivity and success.

Farming is such a slow and gradual process. The farmer doesn't reap the fruits in a day or two; it takes many months of constant care, eventually converting a seed into a tree. The traits in farmers that become crucial are patience, perseverance, and emotional resilience. First and foremost, knowing that the seed will take several months to grow into a tree requires great courage and patience. An entrepreneur's journey is very similar to this gradual process. An entrepreneur also needs to have a similar set of traits: patience is required to see your idea convert into a business, taking care of it at each step, persevering through all the failures and challenges, and still bouncing back not just in terms of business, but emotionally as well, without breaking down.

Through their studies, researchers have shown that approximately 75% of business success is driven by "Emotional intelligence" (EI), which has made it one of the most important skills entrepreneurs should possess to be successful, especially in this world of uncertain challenges[7]. Not just EI, entrepreneurs with good risk-taking abilities are also considered to possess effective stress tolerance, which can create a link between emotional intelligence and optimistic entrepreneurial intentions, along with successful sustenance in entrepreneurial ventures. All the traits, such as emotional maturity, emotional resilience, risk-taking attitude, intuitiveness, decision-making, and stress management, are crucial dimensions of an entrepreneur's personality. They can be linked to the emotional intelligence constructs proposed by Daniel Goleman, like self-awareness, social awareness, self-control, motivation, empathy, and relationship management that guide an entrepreneur through the path full of crises toward the peak of success[7].

Entrepreneurs possess another vital trait closely tied to Emotional Intelligence, *'Creativity.'* A study by Borland in 1975 revealed that creativity is closely linked to emotional stability and high emotional intelligence. This finding underscores the significance of an entrepreneur's personality and psychological traits, as they often distinguish between successful and unsuccessful entrepreneurs[8].

Similar to how a farmer carefully prepares the soil, ensuring it's uneven in some areas and flat in others before sowing seeds, entrepreneurship follows a similar pattern of crests and troughs. However, at the heart of this journey lies a resolute and unwavering "intent," serving as the seed for the farmer and the idea for the entrepreneur.

Farmers, much like entrepreneurs, don't all cultivate the same crops. Some grow crops for personal consumption, while others cultivate commercially for fruits, vegetables, or high-demand products.

Similarly, a study by Zampetakis L.A. et al. (2009) highlighted that the motivation for entrepreneurship is closely tied to one's emotional intelligence (EI)[9]. According to Goleman's EI constructs, motivation is the key component. High levels of EI drive individuals towards embracing risk and novelty, fueling their entrepreneurial pursuits[9].

Among all the other lessons that a farmer teaches us, there is one significant one that, when applied by entrepreneurs in growing their businesses, can aid them in overcoming obstacles and emerging successfully. That lesson is **"Everything can be fixed"**. There are so many machines and equipment that a farmer uses that break down, some suddenly stop working, and some wear and tear over time, but does that stop him from sowing the seeds or reaping the fruits? No. In fact, this inspires him to look for out-of-the-box solutions, such as using drip irrigation instead of letting water flow constantly or replacing the fences with turmeric crops to ward off animals and many others. Entrepreneurs should also remember that things that seem difficult to fix, have a solution. All you need to do is apply some innovative thinking, and then, Aha! the Eureka moment will be right there.

Innovation- The Survival Toolkit for Farmers

Innovation lies at the heart of every Indian agriculture farmer's strategy to tackle many challenges. From enhancing crop production to addressing climate change, from farming dry land in drought-prone areas to alleviating poverty and malnourishment among their families, farmers constantly devise solutions for daunting problems. A simple principle guides their approach: "If we keep doing what we've always done, we'll keep getting the same results. To change the outcomes, we must change our approach and how we tackle challenges." And that is why there is a need for '**innovation-led agricultural growth**.' This growth in agriculture and businesses can only be achieved with the 3 S's – *speed, scale, and sustainability.*

Traditionally, farmers have been strongly pushed to adopt new technology to enhance their farming methods. However, this approach is becoming outdated. Instead, we should foster a culture of 'total innovation,' encompassing technological advancements and institutional innovations across production, marketing, policy research, and enterprise domains. Rather than simply receiving technology, farmers should now become co-creators of knowledge, processes, and innovation, learning through *'collective intelligence'*. To achieve this, we must shift our mindset to '**Doing More from Less Resources for Greater Impact**'[10,] which means maximizing output or productivity while minimizing using resources like land, water, and money to benefit more people, not just to pursue more profit. Land, in particular, presents a challenge for farmers due to high acquisition costs, decreasing per capita availability, and declining quality due to soil erosion, salinity, and waterlogging. To make the most of limited land resources, farmers must harness the potential of cutting-edge technologies, such as information and communication technology, nanotechnology, space technology, and modern biotechnology, alongside innovative policies. For example, using advanced GIS/ GPS and sensors, farmers can monitor groundwater levels to plan irrigation, optimize inputs, and boost yields while reducing water and fertilizer usage.

Mobile apps can provide real-time market information, weather updates, and cultivation trends, empowering farmers to make informed decisions and maximize their productivity despite limited resources.

Collective intelligence can promote a culture of out-of-the-box thinking among all the agriculture stakeholders so that they can innovate devices that reduce long-hauling work and replace it with facile tasks.

For instance, across tea gardens in India, women comprise over fifty percent of the workforce. But for them, manually plucking tea leaves involves much drudgery because of their compulsion to bend their backs for hours. By developing a tea leaf plucking device, the physical health of millions of women can be improved.

Entrepreneurs should not only take lessons from the farmers but also innovate new ideas and technology in agriculture that benefit the farmers and the whole ecosystem. Agritech startups have taken a roaring pace in the startup ecosystem across the globe. Many of them have led to disruption in agriculture through their technology. One of these startups is Nutrifix, which studies the different demands and food preferences of different consumers and, using an AI-based app analyzes this nutritional information to suggest meals to them, which are then purchased by the customers[11].

But what about India? India is no less than these startups launching abroad. Indian entrepreneurs have taken the first step by leveraging technology to innovate ideas in the agricultural sector by creating a market link between the retail, B2C, and B2B marketplaces and digital agronomy platforms[12]. After taking lessons from the farmers, these entrepreneurs have applied them to improve their industry by converging the mobile networks, artificial intelligence, internet bandwidth, cloud platforms, IoT, etc., to create transformational opportunities. Some examples of such trailblazing innovations are BigHaat, a Bengaluru-based startup allowing farmers to buy seeds, crop protection nutrients, fertilizers, other organic solutions, and agro instruments online through its e-commerce platform[13]. Another Indian startup that has grown its roots in Bengaluru is FlyBird Farm Innovations, which uses the technology of sensors put in the soil and helps in the detection of moisture content as well as helps in understanding and fulfilling fertilizer requirements based on the needs of the plant[14]. Ninjacart is another Bengaluru-based startup driven by cutting-edge technology, enabling retailers and merchants to source fruits and vegetables directly from farmers[15]. But it is not just in Bengaluru that the start-up culture is growing; agritech startups such as Ravgo have also established their roots in the state of Punjab by providing the small farmers who cannot afford to own expensive machinery, with a rental marketplace that allows them easy and affordable access to modern technology[16].

An Entrepreneur Who Has Taken the First Step

Kavita Shukla, an inventor and entrepreneur, transformed the shelf life of fruits and vegetables across the globe through her innovation, which she learned during her childhood by observing her maternal grandmother. Her startup, FreshPaper, is helping farmers extend the shelf life of their fruits and vegetables using simple paper sheets infused with powerful organic botanicals that keep fruits and veggies fresh for up to 2-4 times longer[17]. Her idea was sown in the soil during her childhood days when she used to visit her grandmother in India. One day, accidentally, she drank some unfiltered tap water. But instead of giving her any medicine, her grandmother gave her a homemade mixture of spices as a remedy, and because of this, she was saved from getting sick. That turning point sparked her curiosity about how some spices can protect her from the hazardous effects of unfiltered water. After tinkering around her garage with jars of dirty pond water and spices, she gradually discovered that some spices exist that seemingly stop the growth of bacteria and fungus in and around them. This led to the germination of the seed of her idea into a big tree in the form of FreshPaper, which became a new way to keep food fresh longer across the globe[18].

Farmers must adopt an entrepreneurial approach to achieve more significant results with fewer resources, ultimately benefiting more people.

This transition from farmers to "Agripreneurs" marks a fundamental shift in perspective. Rather than solely focusing on increasing productivity, agripreneurs prioritize maximizing Return on Investment (ROI) and profitability, mirroring the mindset of entrepreneurs where profitability holds great significance. With an entrepreneurial mindset, farmers became agripreneurs, taking calculated risks to achieve sustainable profitability and building resilient enterprises. They embrace innovation and experimentation, even in resource-constrained environments. Take Mr. Sadananda, a farmer from Bengaluru, for example. Despite owning a modest 2.1-acre plot of land, he demonstrated the profitability of farming by earning INR 22 lakhs in a year[19]. Mr. Sadananda's success stemmed from his innovative thinking and entrepreneurial skills. Instead of sticking to conventional mono-cropping practices, he diversified his crop portfolio through crop rotation, cultivating nearly 30 different varieties of crops on his small landholding. This strategic shift in cropping patterns allowed him to optimize land usage and maximize returns, showcasing the potential for innovation and entrepreneurship in agriculture. Through his innovative farming practices, Mr. Sadananda has not only boosted his crop yield and profitability but also significantly reduced his overhead expenses, resulting in substantial profits. He allocates half an acre each to cultivate tomatoes and areca, yielding him Rs. 2 lakh and Rs. 50,000, respectively. Additionally, he grows ginger alongside areca, generating around Rs. 70,000 annually. In a clever move, he also raises 250 Giriraja hens, fetching him Rs. 1 lakh every three months. Utilizing poultry droppings as valuable manure for his areca plantation, he closes the loop by feeding plantation waste to the birds. Expanding his agricultural ventures, Mr. Sadananda dedicates three-fourths of an acre to cultivating around 2,000 rose cuttings, yielding an impressive Rs. 4 lakh annually. The remaining one-fourth of his land hosts a greenhouse where he alternates between cultivating capsicum and high-quality roses. Capsicum production generates Rs. 5.4 lakh over six months, while roses contribute Rs. 2.5 lakh annually during the subsequent six months. Mr. Sadananda maintains diversity by incorporating various elements into his farming ecosystem. He maintains a small vegetable garden, a fish-rearing pond enriched with Azolla plants for cattle feed, and coconut and jackfruit trees. With 80 to 100 liters of milk produced daily by his cows, his 2-acre farm mirrors a harmonious blend of agriculture and horticulture. Mr. Sadananda's innovative spirit extends beyond cultivation. He creates his own manure through vermicomposting and slurry obtained from a Gobar gas plant, reducing dependency on borewell irrigation by installing a cost-effective drip irrigation system across his entire land. Furthermore, he breeds Rottweiler and Great Dane dogs, generating an additional income of Rs. 1.2 lakh annually.

Drawing inspiration from agripreneurs like Sadananda, entrepreneurs can learn unconventional thinking and leverage innovation and entrepreneurial skills to reshape the landscape of every industry.

For you, it might be a tiny seed;

what I see in it is a big tree.

Because I am an entrepreneur learning from conventional things,

And applying my innovation to see what magic it brings.

—**Amya Madan**

3.

CREATIVITY

UNLEASHING EARTHWORMS OF ENTREPRENEURIAL INNOVATION

In the words of Albert Einstein, *"Creativity is seeing what others see, but thinking what no one else ever thought."*

To date, the concept of creativity for most people is blurry, elusive, and phantom-like, will-o'-the-wisp, which carries many misconceptions and myths. What makes it more shadowy is that it is difficult to measure in quantifiable units, which means that the degree of people's creativity cannot be defined objectively. But the fact is that all of us possess creativity; while some are born with it naturally, some develop and learn it over time, and others just sit back, thinking they don't need creativity every day.

Now that we have sown our seed of an idea in the soil, it is crucial to beget its growth by putting some creativity into it. Thus, switching to the right brain is paramount to converting an idea into impact through innovation and creative problem-solving. While creativity refers to the fabrication of unique, distinct, and novel ideas in any domain, innovation is concerned with successfully implementing those creative ideas. Creativity is about diverging thinking; innovation is about convergent thinking (Gurteen,

1998)[1]. Creative thinking is more about generating new and out-of-the-box ideas. When one of those ideas becomes reality, it is called 'Innovation.' Just as earthworms, a farmer's best friend, catalyze the germination of the seed in the soil, creative problem-solving also accelerates the growth of an idea to impact. This can be explained further through the 'Three I's Innovation model[2].'

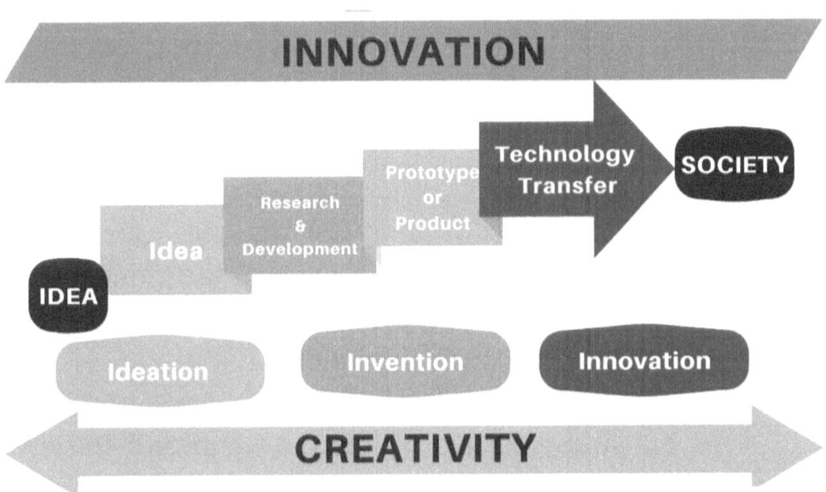

The 3 I's in this model signify Ideation, Invention, and Innovation. However, the journey from Ideation to Innovation includes several other steps. It must undergo a Research and Development (R&D) phase to transform an idea into an innovation. R&D is crucial in advancing ideas toward innovation by fostering knowledge creation within the organization to facilitate inventions (Kabir, 2019)[3]. Additionally, thorough secondary research enables the organization to acquire and assimilate external knowledge, including the knowledge generated by the R&D activities of other organizations (Lane et al., 2006)[4].

Have you ever wondered why earthworms are called farmer's friends? It's pretty simple. They're there for the farmers when nobody else is. Earthworms help farmers in many ways that would be impossible without them. Just by being in the soil, earthworms provide many benefits, like making more plant nutrients available, improving drainage, opening up soil pores for better oxygen flow, and creating a more stable soil structure. All these things help farms produce more crops. Earthworms aren't just friends to farmers; they're also called plowmen of the field, intestines of the earth, ecological engineers, and biological indicators[5]. They're essential for sustainable agriculture because they naturally provide the nutrients that plants need to grow. They're so diverse that they can help manage biodiversity and ecosystem services.

Isn't it similar to how the creative ideas bubbling in an entrepreneur's mind work wonders for their projects, just like earthworms do for farmers? Creativity acts as the plowman of an entrepreneur's mind, digging deep, breaking barriers, and opening up new possibilities. It allows entrepreneurs to think innovatively, solve problems, and generate fresh ideas that drive growth. Like earthworms boost soil health by mixing it up and improving water retention, creativity stirs up an entrepreneur's thoughts, enhancing their ability to innovate and succeed. Earthworms also stimulate microbial activity by thoroughly mixing the soil and water content, thus enhancing the soil's water-holding capacity. Not only the earthworms but their burrows also are channels for plant growth. They act as pathways for root elongation. When earthworms dig burrows, it provides enough space for the roots to elongate within deep soil layers.

Furthermore, this also reduces soil erosion, thereby retaining the moisture in the soil to support plant growth.

Several studies have provided evidence that some earthworms also release specific metabolites, such as vitamin B and vitamin D, into the soil, which are suitable for the growth of plants.

Various studies also report that earthworms can convert barren land into fertile land and increase agricultural output[5]. This is how creative thinking empowers an entrepreneur to envision possibilities beyond the ordinary, fostering the generation of innovative ideas.

AGRICULTURAL LAND IS A FIELD OF UNLIMITED OPPORTUNITIES.

Every day, farmers encounter numerous challenges that demand creative solutions. Their agricultural fields and the market offer countless opportunities for innovation, prompting them to devise novel approaches to tackle everyday problems.

Similarly, entrepreneurs face many problems, pain points, and needs within their market. This environment encourages them to think creatively and develop innovative solutions to address these challenges. Farmers rely on their creativity to build valuable solutions despite operating within constraints. Their strategies are innovative and cost-effective, maximizing the impact of their solutions.

Gone are those days when the farmers used humanoid scarecrows to protect their fields from bird' attacks. Most farmers used to set up scarecrows at several places across their fields to protect their crops from damage caused by birds and other animals. However, they have innovated a low-cost and effective solution to this problem over time without setting up scarecrows.

One such creative solution is linking an iron chain with the motor of a fan.

The fan's motor drives the chain and hits an empty steel box, making a loud noise, which annoys the birds and other animals, so they flee whenever the device emits this constant noise[6]. Another example of farmers adopting innovative solutions in real life is showcased by Anirudh Chaoji, a biologist at Tadoba Andhari Tiger Reserve and director of Ran Mangli Foundation. Ran Mangli is a small village around 70 km from Nagpur, adjoining the beautiful Umred Karhandla Wildlife Sanctuary[7].

In this village, like many others in India, farmers face the persistent problem of wild boars and blue bulls damaging their crops. Despite trying various methods like staying up at night with torches, beating drums, and installing solar panels to scare them off, the farmers found no success. Eventually, they discovered that the animals were frightened by moving objects they could not recognize. In response, the farmers devised a simple and cost-effective solution. They hung colorful plastic bags on nylon ropes spaced evenly around the field. When the wind blew, these bags fluttered and made noise, deterring the animals from entering the fields. However, the animals eventually caught on to this trick and resumed their raids. Undeterred, the farmers found another solution. They observed that the animals avoided turmeric crops. So, they planted turmeric around the perimeter of their fields, creating a natural barrier that kept the wild boars and blue bulls at bay.

Pest control is another major issue that bothers farmers a lot. Many times, the pests are so minuscule that they are not visible to the eyes of the farmers. However, since they are good innovators, one of the farmers came up with the idea of using the stethoscope to detect the presence of pests at an early stage. Just like a stethoscope allows doctors to listen to the heartbeat of patients, this stethoscope can be placed on the outer body of the plant, and when listened to carefully, the farmer can hear the cutting sound of the pests. Accordingly, the required curative measures such as uprooting (removing the plant from the roots out of the soil) or adding pesticides directly to the base of a plant can be taken up after the early detection of pests to protect the affected plants[8].

When discussing creativity, it is equally important to consider its extension in the form of innovation. Startups and businesses worldwide now require a shift from a structured approach, which is too rigid, insular, and expensive, to a more frugal and flexible innovative approach, allowing innovation to happen at a faster, better, and cheaper price. Not just in India but across nations, people have been trained to look for easy-to-use, cheaper ways of doing things using minimum resources since time immemorial. Most innovators in India have a unique mindset called the "Jugaad Mindset." There are six underlying principles of this Jugaad mindset as per the book "Jugaad Innovation" by Navi Radjou, Jaideep Prabhu, and Simone Ahuja[9]. Entrepreneurs can apply these principles to innovate new solutions for their everyday problems. Out of those six, we will discuss the three principles by drawing an analogy between farming and entrepreneurship:

1. **Seek opportunity in adversity:**

    Individuals with a creative mindset don't despair when confronted with challenges. Instead, they view adversity as an opportunity to devise innovative solutions. By embracing adversity as a catalyst for innovation, they endure and flourish in tough circumstances.

    Farmers encounter such challenges in nearly every crop season. Some years bring excessive rainfall, while others suffer from drought. Pests, both small and large, can wreak havoc on crops. However, these adverse conditions prompt farmers to pioneer new farming techniques and methods. Consider the case of Mr. Gadde Satish, a farmer from Andhra Pradesh, who pioneered cattle-based organic farming in response to various challenges such as pest attacks, stagnant crop yields, labor shortages, and high cultivation costs. To address these issues, he introduced open farming practices. During the day, Mr. Satish allows his cattle to graze freely in the fields. He ties the animals in rows across the farm at night using a long rope. He shifts the rope a few meters every other day to give the animals a new resting area. This innovative approach ensures that the dung and urine from the cattle are absorbed directly by the soil, providing natural fertilization. As a result, the soil fertility improves, and weed growth is reduced[10].

Similarly, businesses should also learn to innovate new ways of doing things whenever faced with adversity. Entrepreneurs, business owners, and managers face adversity at every stage during their journey, especially in this competitive world. However, along with having an entrepreneurial mindset, if they are creative problem-solvers as well, then it becomes easier for them to reframe the challenges as opportunities for growth. A creative mindset allows one to change the lens and perceive a challenge as a way to innovate and not get distressed.

At large, if organizations want to succeed, they must make sure that their workforce is resilient. Fred Luthans, professor of Organizational Behavioral psychology, said, "The true value of a company is no longer its tangible assets or even its technological processes, it lies in its human capital & underlying psychological capital – neither of which is open to imitation[11]". Just being innovators themselves would never serve the purpose of an entrepreneur, they must be leaders who can drive, empower, and motivate their employees as well in order to think and act like creative problem-solvers by making them embrace challenges, learn from them, and take steps to overcome those challenges creatively.

2. **Do more with less**

Entrepreneurs need to embrace innovation not only in times of adversity but also in situations of scarcity. While innovation is often associated with competitiveness, its true value lies in supporting high-value employment and fostering inclusive growth. Inclusive growth extends economic opportunities to those who are disadvantaged, integrating them into the economic system as customers, employees, distributors, and intermediaries. By promoting inclusive growth, it can be ensured that resource-poor individuals gain access to essential goods and services at affordable prices; thus inclusive innovation drives positive change and creates opportunities for all members of society to thrive[12]. According to Dr. Mashelkar, former Director General of the Council of Scientific and Industrial Research, the objective of MLM (More from Less for More) type of innovation should not be just to produce low-performance, cheap knock-off versions of high technologies for poor people. Instead, the emphasis should be on harnessing science and high technology to invent, design, produce, and distribute high-performance technologies at prices that can be afforded by the majority of people[12].

Farmers have learned to manage with limited resources to produce the maximum output. Many farmers in India face the issue of land acquisition at a high cost. To add further to the problem is the shortage of labor, which has now started migrating to urban cities for better livelihood opportunities, and then comes the scarcity of resources such as water, pesticides, and fertilizers. Farmers have devised new and creative ways to combat these issues. Due to the scarcity of land, instead of acquiring more land, they have started doing crop rotation to use the field for the entire year by cultivating different crops.

With a change in times, the old notions also change because now it is not necessity that is the mother of invention, but adversity and scarcity, which is the mother of innovation.

Just like a farmer faces scarcity of so many resources while cultivating crops, an entrepreneur, too, during their journey, faces many challenges – sometimes related to the scarcity of funds, human resources, equipment, qualified talent, and even quality customer segments. However, this scarcity acts as a good teacher and allows them to use their creativity to find innovative solutions. For a startup founder, the biggest challenge could be allocating resources to the right department because no matter how much, resources would never be enough in terms of time, people, or money[13]. That doesn't mean that one area of work becomes less important. Instead, it calls for a more innovative approach to prioritize which tasks should be allocated and what amount of resources to raise productivity to the maximum level[14].

Entrepreneurs often perceive time as their most abundant resource when they start their business ventures. Consequently, they tend to stretch their cognitive capacity to its limits. In 2014, Sendhil Mullainathan and Eldar Shafir highlighted in an article that a fixation on scarcity can impair IQ and self-control[15]. The feeling of scarcity or an unmet need can cause a loss of focus and attention, impacting what psychologists refer to as cognitive bandwidth. Cognitive bandwidth encompasses an individual's cognitive capacity, including their ability to pay attention, make sound decisions, stick to plans, and resist distractions while managing other cognitive tasks like planning and initiating actions. Scarcity can significantly affect an individual's cognitive bandwidth, leading to impulsive decision-making rather than rational choices. This phenomenon was demonstrated in a study where two groups of people were tested: one group was asked to memorize a two-digit number, while the other memorized a seven-digit number. Both groups were then asked to wait in an open space, where their decision-making abilities were assessed.

While they were in the waiting area, slices of cake and fruit were displayed in front of them. This was the real test. This experiment was not made to test their memory but their decision-making. The real test was which food they would select while rehearsing those numbers in their mind. The subjects with the two-digit number chose the fruit most of the time. Those whose minds were busy rehearsing the seven-digit number chose the cake 50 percent more often. The cake is an impulsive choice. When our mental bandwidth is used on something else, such as rehearsing digits, we cannot prevent ourselves from making impulsive decisions, here – eating cake[15]. This was proven through this experiment, which is why whenever an entrepreneur's mind is consumed with the thoughts of scarcity, it decreases their overall IQ.

3. **Keep it simple**

The third principle tells the innovator to keep their creative ideas simple. Innovation need not always be technological, highly sophisticated, or a product of thoughtful engineering. It can be simple enough to get a job done effectively and efficiently. Farmers in the field might lack the latest and most advanced technological equipment, but they are full of simple yet novel ideas to innovate and make things easier for them. One such case is of D. Renganathan alias D.N. Venkat, an agriculturist from Coimbatore, Tamil Nadu. He is known to develop a simple yet innovative way of climbing a coconut tree by developing a coconut tree climber with a sitting arrangement, a locking system, and a safety belt[16]. Coconut tree climbers have become rare in Kerala and other coconut-growing states of Karnataka, Tamil Nadu, Andhra Pradesh, Maharashtra, and Goa, with very few taking on the traditional profession. This reluctance among the farmers is because of the high occupational risk as well as the arduous labor involved in climbing tall coconut trees. This further leads to a scarcity of people who could contribute to the coconut farmlands. While observing all these problems, D.N. Venkat designed a simple, low-cost tree climber that addresses all these issues.

He devised a solution with a seating provision and two frames: one upper frame operated by hand and another lower one operated by the leg. The user comfortably sits on the seat, using the up-and-down movement of both frames to climb the tree. A locking system ensures safety, allowing the climber to work fearlessly at any height. A four-lock pin can also be fixed at any level to prevent falls. The device enables climbing up to 40 ft in just 5 minutes, including setup, climbing, and removal.

On the business front, innovators and entrepreneurs should prioritize simplicity in their products and services. This approach offers numerous benefits. Firstly, it maintains high motivation levels as creators can develop quick and cost-effective solutions, making innovations more affordable for customers. Simplicity also ensures ease of maintenance, installation, and use, catering to both skilled and unskilled individuals in the market. This approach fosters inclusive growth, meeting the needs of diverse populations and attracting a broader audience, such as the strategies used by Coke and Pepsi, offering the same products at the same price to everyone. Whether the person is a street vendor or a billionaire, a can of Coke would cost the same to both, unlike the premium products that cater to the needs of only a niche market.

That's why successful businesses spend a great deal of time with their customers, understanding their pain points and observing them, identifying how they can make their products more simple and straightforward. For example, despite significant technological advancements, a large population in India is still stuck in the 2G era, with around

250 million users relying on feature phones that lack internet connectivity[17]. Recognizing this gap in the market, Reliance Jio identified an opportunity to empower every Indian with the benefits of digital services, particularly those who couldn't afford smartphones. Reliance Jio launched the Jio Bharat Phone, an affordable internet-enabled phone designed to bridge the digital divide and provide access to essential online services to millions of feature phone users across India. Priced at just ₹999, it offers the lowest entry price for an internet-enabled phone[18]. With a 1.77-inch QVGA TFT display, HD calling, and support for UPI payments and OTT services, the phone delivers a seamless user experience[19]. Jio identified the demand for affordable internet-enabled phones among feature phone users and responded with a tailored solution, thus exemplifying Reliance Jio's commitment to understanding and addressing the needs of its customers.

There could be several other principles governing the Jugaad innovation, but if thought about well, these three principles can guide the thinking of most innovations. Recognizing that financial constraints and limited resources are forms of scarcity is crucial. In times of adversity and shortage, efficient management of cognitive bandwidth is critical to fostering innovation in the workplace. Working excessively long hours, pushing oneself harder, and sacrificing leisure time will not necessarily boost productivity. Instead, it can overextend the cognitive capacity to the point where there's little room for creativity to flourish in the mind.

Psychiatrists have reported an increasing number of patients who show symptoms of acute stress, which is caused by a stretch to their limits and beyond, with no margin, no room in their lives for rest, relaxation, and reflection[15]. There is nothing magical about working tirelessly for 50 or 60 hours a week. However, there is indeed something magical and essential about letting your mind out for a jog, on vacation, or at least a good sleep—to maximize cognitive and creative bandwidth rather than hours worked.

Meet my friends, those tiny earthworms, crawling in the soil,

Fueling my mind with innovation, making creativity boil.

When a farmer sleeps, they tirelessly work in the field,

To catalyze the growth and for the best yield.

– Amya Madan

PART 2

GROWTH OF SAPLING = ESTABLISHING A STARTUP

4.

THE ART OF GROWTH

LESSONS FROM THE BONSAI TREE

Nature does not hurry, yet everything is accomplished.

– Lao Tzu

A viable seed, when sown well, will show its magic by sprouting out from the soil as a small and delicate sapling. After months of absorbing nutrients, watering the soil, providing sufficient sunlight, and required fertilizers, farmers see the first glimpse of their efforts tangibly in the form of a sapling. Nevertheless, this requires constant belief as well as enormous patience.

As a seedling grows into a big tree in a rainforest, an entrepreneur nurtures their idea till it reaches the stage of a **Minimum Viable Product (MVP)** – the initial fruit of their labor. MVP is the simplest version of your product that you can quickly build and test with real customers. It's like a sneak peek or a trial version of your final product. The goal is to get feedback from users early on, so you can learn what they like and don't like before investing too much time and money into making the full product. For example, you want to bake a cake, but you're not sure what flavor everyone will like. Instead of spending hours baking a full cake with all the toppings, you make a small batch of cupcakes first. These cupcakes are your Minimum Viable Product (MVP). So, instead of spending months developing a complex product that may or may not meet the customers' needs, startups create an MVP to test their ideas and gather feedback. This allows them to make improvements based on real user experiences, ultimately increasing their chances of success when they launch the final product.

Though a seed takes 2-4 weeks to grow into a sapling, the maturity of the sapling may take 6-8 weeks. This duration also exists for startups when entrepreneurs feel they have found their eureka moment of knowing which idea they have to work on, but that requires constant care, support, nurturing, good governance, creativity, and strategic decision-making. With all this in place, the idea becomes mature enough to be converted into a **Proof of Concept (POC)** and then into a **Minimum Viable Product (MVP)** before it can be grown into a big tree (launch the product).

The primary purpose of a POC is to validate the technical feasibility or viability of a concept or idea. It aims to answer the question, "Can this idea be implemented?" It focuses on demonstrating the concept's core functionality or specific feature. Once the technical feasibility is assessed, the idea then moves to the MVP stage. The primary purpose of an MVP is to validate the market demand and gather feedback from real users. It aims to answer the question, "Is there a need for this product, and will people use it?" It focuses on delivering the minimum set of features required to solve a specific problem for users.

A POC involves building a small-scale prototype or demonstration to showcase the technical feasibility of an idea. It may not include all the features or functionalities of the final product and is often limited to testing a specific aspect of the concept. However, an MVP is a functional version of the product that includes the minimum set of features required to address the target market's needs. It is developed with the intention of releasing it to real users to gather feedback and iterate based on their responses.

Not every seed flourishes into a rainforest, just as not every idea blossoms into a thriving business. While bonsai and rainforests are starkly different, each imparts unique lessons for business growth. The diversity in their growth trajectories underscores the importance of recognizing value in all stages of development, whether modest or monumental. This means that even those startups with stunted growth still hold much economic value.

As a seed finds suitable conditions for its growth, it germinates into a sapling by breaking itself to sprout, which anchors the sapling and enables it to absorb water from the soil. After the root, the next part that grows is the shoot, which then transforms to grow leaves, stems, trunks, etc.

However, some plants exist that do not grow into a tree, not tall or big but mature enough to sustain over years.

How? What does this signify? Is growing tall and branching out the only sign of success?

Not really. A Bonsai defies this theory, it has been sustained over the years yet has not grown tall.

Though Bonsai plants typically remain below 4 feet tall, some can live up to 1,000 years because, though they might look delicate, they can be the most resilient given proper care[1].

During the pandemic, I developed an interest in gardening, finding solace in nurturing plants, from seed to bonsai. However, I soon discovered that caring for a bonsai is a delicate art that requires constant attention. It is a balancing act: ensuring the right amount of sunlight, water, and pruning to keep the bonsai thriving.

I meticulously monitored my bonsai's environment daily, mindful of its sunlight exposure to prevent scorching or withering. I carefully watered it, mindful not to drown its delicate roots. Regular pruning is essential, so I removed dead leaves and branches to stave off disease.

What fascinated me the most was the versatility of bonsai cultivation. While there are specialized "dwarf trees," I learned that any plant can be transformed into a bonsai with patience, skill, and dedicated care. Ultimately, the success of a bonsai's growth rests in the hands of the caretaker.

Talking about the limited growth of Bonsai, their constricted height, delicacy, etc., might sound like an analogy to the stunted growth of a startup. However, in the true sense, these bonsai can provide significant business lessons, which they have taught Japanese businesses for years.

Do not judge bonsai trees by their size alone; their resilience holds the secret to the enduring power of Japanese businesses. Growing and maintaining a bonsai isn't a walk in the park. It demands precise care—pruning at the right time and shaping, adequate watering, constant attention, and ample sunlight. Plus, the right pot size and soil type are crucial.

Pruning isn't just about looks; it's vital for the bonsai's longevity. Pruning breathes life into the bonsai by trimming away dead branches and encouraging new growth. Water content and soil quality play pivotal roles, too. Bonsai trees need regular watering, but soggy soil spells trouble as it can lead to root rot. That's why well-draining soil with gravel, sand, or pebbles is preferred for bonsai cultivation.

Given proper care and individual attention, any entrepreneur can convert their idea into a startup with a strong drive and constant determination, just as any plant can be converted into a bonsai. The business need not be a conglomerate company, but it can be as simple as selling juice through a kiosk built in front of one's lawn. This is, technically, a business. However, the success of this business boils down to how well you manage it. Japanese businesses have been learning management from the Bonsai for years and sustaining their business over centuries.

In 2019, over 33,000 businesses in Japan were over a century old, according to research firm Teikoku Data Bank[2]. There are century-old businesses and shops in Japan, such as the Nishiyama Onsen Keiunkanopen, the oldest hotel in the world. Fifty-two generations of the same family have run it, and it has hosted guests since 705 AD. Some other businesses are the Ichimonjiya Wasuke, the Kyoto-based confectioner selling sweets since 1000, and well-known technology businesses like Nintendo, which has a sprawling history and has been in business since 1889. Compared to these Japanese businesses, 76% of UK FTSE 100 companies have disappeared in the last 30 years[3].

The question is, what is Japan's secret sauce to business longevity? The Bonsai plant has the answer to this. Various unique practices need to be followed while growing a bonsai that has been acting as a guide to Japanese companies for several years and is the secret sauce to their business longevity.

In order to grow a bonsai in a specific shape, it is pruned in the correct form and is wired appropriately. Proper discipline and prudence are required to prune the bonsai properly. That means it requires a high level of attention, which forms the heart of the Japanese business mentality. That is how most hospitality businesses in Japan differentiate themselves from the rest of the world through *Omotenashi*, which refers to their specific approach to hospitality, where they value the customers' needs much before they ask for it. "Omote" means public face – an image you wish to present to outsiders. "Nashi" means nothing. Combining them means every service is from the bottom of the heart – honest, no hiding, no pretending[4].

By being transparent with the customers and building moments of appreciation and trust, customer loyalty can be increased in business, but this requires a great deal of attention to focus on the customer feedback and their behavior, as well as differentiating between what is essential and what is not. Bonsai plants are also known to have a longer life if carefully maintained over generations.

There are several long-living Bonsai that have stayed strong for centuries. The Ficus Bonsai tree at Crespi, Italy, is the oldest Bonsai, over 1000 years old[5]. Many other such long-living Bonsai have overcome the ravages of time and destruction and have survived because of how they were grown and nurtured by their caretakers. Not only did the Bonsai live for over 500 years, but they were also nurtured for several years. For example, the Yamaki family tamed the Japanese White Pine for over six generations[5], meaning the Bonsai was nurtured for over 400 years. Because of the patience and hard work of this family, the Bonsai tree could survive the Hiroshima atomic bomb attack in 1945, which makes it even more special. Such is the beauty of a Bonsai, and Japanese companies have learned to distinguish themselves by their ability to withstand the vehemence of time. According to a report published by the Bank of Korea in 2008, out % of the 5,586 companies older than 200 years in 41 countries, 56% of them were in Japan[6]. Most Japanese companies have achieved this because they prioritize long-term value over short-term gains. Instead of strategizing their business models and creating visions for five or ten years down the line, they think more about how they want the future to look like 100 or 200 years from now. Entrepreneurs should also possess far-sightedness so that they not only think about the needs of the present-day people, but also future generations. Japanese companies, in this regard, think with a long-term mindset. This vision is mirrored in the fact that only 1% of waste in Japan ends up in landfills, and in the global transition to renewables, Japan currently ranks at number five in the world[7]. They bestow great importance on the long-term health of future stakeholders. Like a nurturer who dutifully waters a bonsai tree to advance it to their offspring, startup founders should not just build for themselves but also innovate and invest for future generations.

BONSAI FOR BOUNDLESS BUSINESSES

Though it looks like a small plant, with little growth and not bearing fruits or any flowers, bonsai can still provide lessons that can be applied to create boundless businesses w.r.t to time, innovation, and growth. Careful observation is essential for growing the Bonsai. Ignoring it for some days could either make it grow in a distorted shape and size or can even hamper its life.

In the same way, startup founders should be careful and observant while they take days off from work because even when they are not in business, the world around them is still providing them with cues and insights to innovate and reinvent their products/services. Pruning is essential for plants as much as cutting down on costs, time and errors are for startups. Though it looks good to see a plant grow how it wants to, pruning them makes them as valuable as a Bonsai. Entrepreneurs should use technology in such a way that they can improve the processes so that it helps the employees perform better by saving money (affordable), reducing cycle time (rapid), and also minimizing errors (excellence). Pruning for startups works on reducing cost, time, and errors to generate maximum value and a high return on investment.

BRANDING THROUGH BONSAI

The Bonsai story isn't just about growing tiny trees; it's a valuable lesson for startups and companies shaping their brand strategies. Like a bonsai needs regular and precise watering to thrive, brands must consistently meet their customers' needs. "Bonsai" means "planted in a container" in Japanese. Bonsai growers often change pots to encourage denser root growth and provide fresh environments for their plants to flourish.

Similarly, brands must adapt and evolve quickly to stay relevant and avoid falling behind[8].

LEADING PEOPLE, JUST LIKE THE BONSAI PLANT.

While we have been talking much about metaphorizing bonsai and applying lessons to startups, it is also essential to dive deep into how these lessons from the bonsai plant can help create leadership traits in an entrepreneur. These lessons are needed because it is not just enough to start a business but to manage a team as well. Just like a randomly growing tree, teams are also imperfect. However, they can be shaped into valuable bonsai plants by the bonsai "grower," the leader. Leaders should have a unique amalgamation of grace and courage to shape their people. There are many qualities that a leader can learn from the bonsai plant. Instead of fixing people's weaknesses, leaders should focus on honing their strengths[9]. A bonsai artist looks for the distinctiveness of their plants, which they can showcase, and based on that, they shape the bonsai into an artistic marvel. Focusing on employees' weaknesses would fabricate nothing; the strengths produce results.

Successful startups are not built in a day; they require years of patience, hard work, and dedication, just like it takes decades and generations to create a perfect bonsai. There are no shortcuts to producing growth.

Four centuries make that tree what it is[10]. A leader should always be individualistic while dealing with each team member. For a skilled bonsai grower, not all trees are alike. He knows the time and season for pruning a trident maple are different from a juniper.

In the same way, people are also unique and different. That is why a leader should be considerate while dealing with each of them. A bonsai master believes that pruning is very important for growing the bonsai perfectly. Pruning involves removing the unwanted branches or sometimes the entire limb, just to maintain the bonsai's health. Leaders should remove those challenges and hurdles that are stopping the employees in the organization from reaching their full potential.

Through the bonsai's journey, we learn that greatness is not measured by size but by the depth of character and the ability to thrive in adverse conditions. Let's apply these lessons to our own ventures with the same reverence and dedication as the bonsai master, knowing that with perseverance and care, even the smallest seed has the potential to grow into something extraordinary.

Growing up in a shallow container, I was finite yet valuable

Bonsai they call me – artistic and infallible.

Learn from my story, how enduring I am because of my master's care,

You too can nurture your startup, only if you can dare.

– Amya Madan

5.

VITAMIN M

MENTORSHIP & MONEY AS NUTRIENTS FOR SUCCESS

*"Mentoring is a brain to pick, an ear to listen,
and a push in the right direction."*

– John C. Crosby

Just like nurturing a bonsai requires a delicate balance of care, protection, water, and sunlight, a seed needs the right mix of fertilizers and nutrients to sprout and grow into a healthy plant. Each nutrient plays a crucial role, and deficiencies can hinder growth or even cause the plant to wither prematurely. That is why, a seed needs timely nourishment to thrive and reach its full potential.

Among many other nutrients that plants need, the three most important are Nitrogen (N), Phosphorus (P), and Potassium (K), abbreviated as NPK[1]. All these nutrients benefit the plant in different ways and help in its maturation. Nitrogen gives the plant, its dark green color which reflects in the color of its leaves and also promotes growth. In addition to Nitrogen, plants require Phosphorus which helps in the elongation and growth of roots, as well as provides protection to the plants from diseases. Phosphorus also helps the plants in producing flowers and seeds. Potassium is the third important nutrient constantly required by plants. Just like Phosphorus, Potassium also protects plants from diseases and encourages root growth. Potassium is also necessary for plants to make chlorophyll which is a pigment that provides a green color to the plants. Apart from these three primary nutrients, there are some secondary nutrients as well which are required by the plants. These are Calcium, Magnesium, and Sulphur. Besides these, plants also require other nutrients, albeit in smaller quantities. These nutrients which are essential for plant growth but required in small quantities are called "trace nutrients" which are Iron (Fe), Manganese (Mn), Zinc (Zn), Copper (Cu), Boron (B), Molybdenum (Mo), and Chloride (Cl)[2].

In total, there are about 17 different nutrients that are essential for the growth and development of plants and each of them plays a specific role & function[3]. Not all nutrients are taken up by the plants through the same channel, three of these nutrients are taken up from the water and air, while the remaining nutrients are absorbed by the roots in the soil. Despite the presence of nutrients in the soil, plants still need fertilizers to meet their nutritional deficiency because a lot of these nutrients get washed away by rainfall or during floods.

You must be wondering, I am not a farmer, I am an entrepreneur. Why should I know all of this?

Well! Because, similar to how a farmer supplements soil with nutrients to nourish seeds into thriving plants, an entrepreneur requires mentorship as a vital element to cultivate and develop their startup idea. Just as each nutrient serves a specific purpose for plant growth, mentorship from individuals with diverse backgrounds and expertise is essential for shaping an idea into a viable business.

Like some plants form symbiotic relationships with fungi to enhance nutrient absorption, entrepreneurs benefit from mutual mentorship exchanges. In these relationships, both parties contribute and receive valuable insights and support. This symbiosis is beneficial in challenging environments, where collaboration can help startups flourish despite adversity. The plants that take help from fungi to absorb more nutrients from the soil don't just take up but always give back, making it a two-way transaction. In exchange for the help they receive in absorbing nutrients, plants share some of their sugars with the fungi as food and provide them with a space to live. These mycorrhizal ('myco' meaning fungi, 'rhizae' meaning root) relationships are primarily found in areas where soil quality is poor, thus proving beneficial to the plants. In the same way, mentorship is not only about marching up to a mentor and taking advice but also a two-sided relationship built on mutual trust and natural connectedness, not forced by any external factor.

Anthony Tjan, during one of his TEDxBeaconStreet, talked about five types of mentors that one should have around them to accelerate the growth and development of ideas and emerge as industry leaders[4]. Just like a plant needs some primary nutrients essential for its growth, these mentors are also integral for the growth of a startup.

1. The first mentor is the **"Master of Craft"**: These are the people who are the best in their specific fields, be it the most iconic football player or an exemplary writer, the most successful entrepreneur, or the most prolific editor. These people can be the guiding masters who have accumulated knowledge through their experience of several years. Thus, they can provide insights into what can go wrong during the journey and how to make it right through self-improvement. These should be go-to mentors whenever advice is needed about initiating a new startup

or brainstorming solutions because they can quickly help identify and realize one's strengths and hone them to reach the closest state of perfection.

2. Another vital nutrient (mentor) for the growth of your idea is the "**Champion of your cause**." These mentors act as the power boosters for the founder and their startup because, through their network, they can easily connect them to industry-relevant people. These people act as advocates supporting the cause one is trying to solve through their ideas.

3. The third essential mentor is the "**Copilot**," and as the name says, these are the people who are your best work buddies. A co-pilot can be anybody: a co-founder, a close friend, or a colleague with whom one can discuss and debate whatever is going on in one's mind and who can also guide navigating through the challenges just by listening to the dilemmas over a coffee. However, these mentorships work best when they are mutual with equal reciprocal. It is more like a collaborative mentorship where each one supports the other and holds the other accountable, eventually upgrading the quality of work through constant engagement.

4. Another essential mentor is called "**Anchor**", the people who hold you firm when you are stumbling. These people could be anyone, a friend or family member. While a champion provides support by guiding one to achieve the targeted goals, an anchor acts as a confidante, the sounding board when uncertainties crawl in or when there are speed breakers in one's growth and development. These people help convert those stumbling blocks into stepping stones by providing emotional support and psychologically uplifting one's mood so that instead of seeing the walls in the confinement of a room, one sees the light through the

cracks between them. They are crucial because they help align goals and priorities, balancing work targets and life's enjoyment.

5. Last but certainly, not least are the "**Reverse mentors**". These people might not fit into the typical category of mentors but are crucial for providing insights that sometimes get missed. Typically, the personality figure of a mentor is considered to be someone who is well-versed in the subject knowledge, an older person, a teacher, or a professor. But we sometimes miss to notice that even the little kids playing around can be mentors who, in their innocent ways, can teach a lot. Launching a startup is not a destination; it is a journey, and during this journey, there are many ups and downs that one has to face. Talking to the younger generation can allow one to gather insightful feedback, be updated with the latest changing trends, and build a fresh perspective of looking at things in the Gen-Z way.

Some nutrients help plants in transpiration, some in disease resistance, and others in flowering and respiration. Similarly, mentors play a crucial role in various ways to help start-ups grow from the seed of an idea. Mentors, through their immense knowledge and experience, can provide valuable insights. The experience of mentors allows them to share deeper discernment about what challenges one might encounter while walking on the journey of building one's venture. As the nurturer of an entrepreneurial baby, one might sometimes miss out on looking at it from a critical point of view. That's where a mentor can provide a new and fresh perspective through critical feedback. Mentors also gently hold their mentees' hands, helping them discover their true potential and further guide them to grow and succeed.

And while we are talking about the role of mentors in helping one reach their highest potential, here is what my mentor, Dr. R.A. Mashelkar, taught me and I quote, "There is no limit to human endurance, no limit to human imagination, no limit to human achievements, except the limits you will put on to yourself. When Tenzing Norgay and Edmund Hillary conquered Everest in 1953, the feat was considered to be impossible. But once it was shown that it was possible, there have been close to 6000 conquests! And impossible-looking feats have been done. Someone has climbed Everest 21 times, someone has climbed it without supplemental oxygen, an eighty-year-old has climbed it as also a young boy and a girl (each of age less than fourteen) have climbed it, a blind person, a double leg amputee, and a double arm amputee have climbed it! So there is no limit to human achievement. If they could do it, you could do it too[5]."

ALONG WITH NUTRIENTS, PLANTS REQUIRE VITAMIN-M TOO.

As much as startups require mentorship, they also require money from bootstrapping or angel funding. Plants can uptake nutrients from the soil, but many of these nutrients either get washed away, are depleted, or can vanish after harvesting. Farmers use fertilizers in their fields to replenish this loss of nutrients to provide plants with the required nutrients, thus fertilizers are integral in rejuvenating the soil.

Fertilizers are saviors for plants whenever they require nutrients to perform a specific function. A plant nutrition consultant, Barry Bullltant said, "Without fertilizers, the soil would be depleted and therefore plants would be particularly difficult to grow. They cannot survive on water alone, and nor can we[6]." Fertilizers ensure that crops yield greater by fulfilling the nutrient deficiencies in plants. For the startups, the angel investors are analogous to these fertilizers. The angel investors provide the most critical Vitamin-M (money) when the startups need additional funds. Angel investors are those individuals who invest in entrepreneurial ventures using their capital in exchange for equity. They often provide startup founders with the capital for their business, but they do not have any operational voting rights in the company[7]. Through their network and expertise, angel investors can also provide credibility to the startup.

Thus, each nutrient plays a crucial role, and their deficiencies can hinder growth or cause the plant to wither prematurely. Similarly, an entrepreneur needs mentorship as a vital element to cultivate and develop their startup idea. Just as plants require nutrients and fertilizers to thrive, startups require mentorship and funding to succeed in the competitive business landscape.

Lost I was, uncertain and unsure,

My mentor devoured me from questions and became my source of cure.

Just like that tiny sapling, up taking nutrients through diffusion,

Accelerated my growth, setting aside all confusion.

– Amya Madan

6.

WEATHERING THE STORM

BUILDING RESILIENT STARTUPS

"The only way to win is to learn faster than anyone else."

– Eric Ries

After nurturing the seeds for months, meticulously preparing the soil, regulating temperature and climate, and ensuring the provision of essential nutrients, the seed finally breaks through the surface, germinating into a fragile seedling. This initial sapling is the farmer's first glimpse of the fruition of their efforts. However, with growth comes vulnerability. The seedling germinates from the soil and enters a world fraught with uncertainties and harsh environmental conditions. This delicate growth phase is pivotal, as the young plant must adapt to its new surroundings, braving heavy rains, strong winds, and wildlife threats. Now, the farmer's responsibilities multiply, as they must shield their saplings from potential harm, nurturing them into sturdy trees capable of bearing fruit. While crops rely on adequate rainfall for sustenance, excessive downpours can prove detrimental, damaging delicate seedlings and jeopardizing the entire season's harvest. Over the years, farmers have dealt with these challenges. Through experimentation, they have developed innovative strategies for safeguarding their precious seedlings against adverse weather conditions, including fierce winds, torrential rains, and even hailstorms.

Entrepreneurs can face a similar situation while converting their ideas into their businesses. Until the idea is theirs, they can mold it how they want to, and it will be protected. However, the day the idea comes out into the market among the customers, after the launch of the product/service, it is no longer only theirs. Entrepreneurs' task now increases to protect their ideas from critics and competitors. The launched products, services, or processes need not just be protected from the competitors but also need to grow parallelly. That is why the strategies of an entrepreneur should be such that they neither limit the growth and expansion of their startups nor get overpowered by the competition.

Farmers can't stop rain or cease thunderstorms or colds. However, the least they can do to protect their crops from damage is to control and reduce the impact of these environmental ravages.

Often, farmers, especially those who plant tomatoes, face this issue because of a mismatch in the timings of sowing the seeds. Farmers have found creative and innovative ways to protect the tomato plant's fresh, grown, delicate saplings from the wreck of the cold breeze and frost at night. They either create a bell-shaped jar-like structure covering the crop, called a cloche, or they create plastic/fabric row covers in the entire field to protect the crops[1]. Indian farmers have also devised easy ways of creating these plastic cloches with the help of plastic barrels, such as removing their bottoms to protect the saplings from frost. Instead of covering each sapling with a cloche, row covers allow the farmers to group several saplings or plants to protect them. The farmers are also thoughtful about saplings needing sunlight, so they remove these cloches and row covers during the morning when the sun is bright, and there is no frost to allow the plants to make food.

Plants can be their guardians, too. Farmers often set up windbreaks to shield young saplings from being blown away by strong winds. These windbreaks act like barriers, lessening the force of the wind, keeping the soil in place, and preventing erosion. Farmers plant rows of tall, sturdy trees around their fields to create a windbreak. These trees form a protective shield against strong winds and heavy rains. Typically, there are two rows of trees: one with more giant trees and another with smaller ones. This setup helps reduce the impact of wind and rain, safeguarding the delicate saplings as they grow.

Heavy rainfall can damage the leaves of the plants. To protect the crops from the devastating effects of rain, they use a fabric net or covering in the shape of a tubelike structure, thus protecting the leaves from directly getting in contact with the raindrops. Various startups are already working in this direction of creating ready-to-use equipment for farmers to help them protect their crops. For example, mesh4 has created a windbreak using metallic wires, which protects by reducing the force of the strong winds and rainfall[2].

These instances of the agricultural world are relevant because they can act as a lesson for growing startups in their most fragile state when they launch their product or service in the market. Every day, startups face new challenges, whether competition from big players or critics and competitors in the same field. The devastating effects of the winds and rainfall make farmers look for more innovative ideas.

Similarly, the competition makes startups more innovative and progressive. Though competition is terrible, so are the winds, storms, and frost, there is no way one can avoid it. The only thing that can be done is to reduce the impact – not hamper the startup's growth. Farmers know exactly when the season changes by keeping track of different environmental signals.

In the same way, as an entrepreneur, one should keep track of the competition in the market. It is essential to focus more on the brand identity and keep the needs and preferences of the customers as the top priority. However, knowing what the rivals are doing is equally important, as it helps prepare future steps and strategies.

By focusing on understanding and meeting the needs of their customers, startups can discover their competitive edge and unique value proposition which can serve as the most robust defense against challenges from competitors. This competitive advantage acts as a shield, safeguarding the growing startup from the negative impacts of competition on its sales and revenue. Like a cloche protecting young saplings, the competitive advantage shields the startup by offering something different from the norm in the market. This uniqueness leads to disruptive innovations, shaking up the industry and leaving competitors struggling. Netflix faced a similar situation in the Blockbuster era. Blockbuster was founded in 1985 as a VHS Rental Company and was considered the McDonald's of movie rentals. Around 2006, Netflix emerged, making just a mere $1 billion in revenue that year, which was relatively short of Blockbuster's revenue of roughly $5.5 billion[3]. In 2007, Netflix introduced a unique proposition of streaming video, which allows viewers to watch films on their home computers. This feature set it apart from Blockbuster's offerings, leading to its steady decline and bankruptcy.

Entrepreneurs must move swiftly, like lightning, to navigate the competitive landscape while attentively listening to their customers' discussions. By actively listening to their customers' concerns, suggestions for enhancements, and desires for improvements to existing systems, entrepreneurs can innovatively craft solutions to address these challenges. This proactive approach enables entrepreneurs to develop a distinctive value proposition for their products and services, setting them apart in the market.

Not only do the startups face competition from the big players in the market, but sometimes the big, established companies also face competition from the new players and startups emerging in the market. A recent example of this competition was discussed by Abhishek Patil, Founder of GrowthX, who mentioned the steep decline in the sales revenue of companies like Mondelez, Mars, Nestle, Perfetti Van Melle, Parle & ITC since 2020[4]. While the pandemic led to the digitization of the whole commerce industry, where UPI became a game-changer, it negatively affected the sales of toffee manufacturing companies such as Parle, Nestle, etc.

Back in 2010, 'chhutta' (money change) in the form of candies dominated the local grocery and general stores. In the absence of change in exchange for the money paid by the customers, the shopkeepers used to give them the toffees or candies. However, UPI killed this candy business. Hershey's, one of the world's most prominent chocolate and toffee makers, said that the Indian market in the post-COVID era is hitting their expansion plan[5]. Before the pandemic, few people used the UPI (Gpay, PhonePay, or Paytm). The easiest and the most convenient way of transaction used to be cash, which was preferred not only by the customers but also by the shopkeepers because no change was their additional source of revenue, which further added to the revenue of big toffee players. However, with the pandemic, UPI became the most convenient source of transactions, allowing customers not to carry any cash. However, this led to a steep decline in the sales of the toffees because customers now started paying the exact amount of money, leaving the need for a "change" almost negligible. Thus, another point to note is that the competitors may or may not be from the same industry.

Who would have thought that the biggest competitor for a toffee company would be a fin-tech product?

However, it is also essential to understand that here, the industry is not a competition; the behavior or requirements of the customers play a significant role. Many customers did not buy toffees but used them as cash substitutes, so the competition came from the fintech company, not the food industry. UPI did not replace the toffees directly but indirectly by changing people's behavior.

A farmer who wants to protect the crops from the impact of the frost cannot install windbreaks in their field. Similarly, those who want to protect their saplings from rainfall cannot use windbreaks.

Thus, the source and reason for the threat are significant before protecting the crops. This example showcases a crucial lesson for startups and established enterprises: understanding the underlying reasons driving consumer purchases is paramount.

By understanding consumer behavior patterns, startups can decipher the factors influencing fluctuations in their sales figures. Whether observing a decline or surge in sales, tapping into consumer insights can enable businesses to make informed decisions about their products or services.

Startups need to understand that technology is the key to unlocking the potential of their offerings in today's world. Better technology provides a competitive edge for startups to accelerate their growth. Sun Tzu said, "Keep your friends close; keep your enemies closer[6]." This phrase can prove to be true for entrepreneurs because they should keep a close eye on their competitors' new moves and marketing gimmicks. Tracking their sales and revenue can help determine future strategies. We are in a fantastic era of innovation, with startups and businesses ripping up norms and bringing value to consumers through more choice and utility. However, many startups fail because they believe "If you build it, they will come." This leads to startups being outmaneuvered in their markets by not considering how to win a competitive advantage[7].

Farmers sometimes dig a long, wide channel around the area where their crops are sown to prevent excessive flood water from destroying the crop. A similar moat needs to be built by the startups around them, which can act as their shield and protect them from competitors. However, the moat for them is their competitive advantage, enabling them to strengthen their brands while maintaining customer loyalty through reasonable pricing, marketing strategies, and legal protections. A marketplace network is a good way for startups to build a durable competitive advantage. This could be made possible by bringing together customers and suppliers in a marketplace. It is like creating an aggregator system where the demand and supply create a self-reinforcing cycle of growth built on network effects. With more suppliers joining the marketplace, there is more supply. Thus, its demand increases, reducing prices and drawing in more customers. More suppliers join as customers are drawn to the marketplace for its quality or low prices, driving further competition and growth[8].

A ray of light emerges from the leaves, trapped in a sheltered container,

Knowing it's important for growth, protecting them from winds through this strainer.

While startups continue to find their ray of hope amidst their competitor,

Their protector is their value proposition, acting as their sustainer.

— Amya Madan

7.

THRIVING TOGETHER
COLLABORATION OVER COMPETITION

If you want to be incrementally better, be competitive

If you want to be exponentially better, be collaborative.

Plants possess a fascinating hidden world beyond their visible structures. While we typically perceive plants as living organisms due to their ability to breathe, move, and produce their own food, their complexity extends further. Plants exhibit behaviors akin to feeling, collaboration, and competition, demonstrating an understanding of their environment similar to human beings. Just as an entrepreneur aspires for the growth of their business, plants, too, strive to outgrow their neighbors. They sense and respond to their surroundings, often competing for resources like sunlight. This competition is evident above ground, where plants may grow taller or spread out to block each other's access to sunlight. Yet, beneath the surface lies a hidden competition unfolding in the soil.

Let's see how plants compete for resources and tackle competition around them. Uproot a plant, and you will notice a bunch of roots. Many times, the roots of the plants are concentrated just below their shoot vertically, while in other instances, they also spread their roots horizontally, foraging for nutrients and water. Not all plants grow equal volume or density of roots; instead, their "investment" in roots depends upon the total volume of roots produced and how they are distributed throughout the soil[1].

In a greenhouse at the Museo Nacional de Ciencias Naturales (CSIC) in Madrid, researchers conducted a fascinating experiment on pepper plants to investigate their behavior and responses during competition[1]. The objective was to understand how plants adapt underground when grown alone versus when they have neighboring plants. The findings of this study offered intriguing insights.

The study revealed that when pepper plants were grown near each other, they showed a localized increase in root investment, with a greater concentration of roots growing vertically below the shoot. They also displayed reduced horizontal root expansion to avoid overlapping with neighboring plants. Thus, plants focused more on increasing their own fitness by increasing investment in the volume of their roots vertically instead of spreading far for resources. Conversely, when the plants were spaced further apart, they invested less in their roots compared to solitary conditions.

Just as plants compete for resources underground, startups and organizations also face competition while establishing themselves, scaling up, or expanding globally. However, rather than engaging in unnecessary rivalry, they can benefit from enhancing their fitness, value propositions, and competencies. By doing so, they can mitigate unnecessary competition and accelerate their individual growth trajectories.

The water and minerals beneath the soil are analogous to an organization's customers, clients, and potential buyers. While everyone desires to attract more of them, it's impractical to capture them all. Instead, it's wiser to channel energy and resources into deepening roots, strengthening core competencies, and focusing on acquiring targeted customers. This strategic approach fosters substantial growth. Conversely, attempting to encroach on the territory of others yields no benefits. Similarly, startups benefit more from targeting a niche market segment and investing in its acquisition rather than engaging in broad competition with all surrounding competitors.

There are situations when plants also have to deal with abiotic stressors (water, nutrients, carbon dioxide, etc.) and biotic stressors (outbreaks of insects, predators, etc.). Especially in resource-poor habitats, plants compete for nutrients, water, space, pollinators, etc. A lot of times, this competition occurs between the plants and other small micro-organisms, but there are instances of competition occurring between two plants as well, which could be in the form of inter-specific competition between different species of similar and different life forms (e.g., woody vs. herbaceous) and intra-specific competition (e.g., adult vs. juvenile)[2].

However, for startups, competition shouldn't be the primary concern. The truth is that most startups don't make it. While some falter due to being outpaced by competitors, a study by CB Insights revealed that competition ranks as the fourth most common reason for startup failure[3]. But it's not the sole culprit. Surprisingly, lack of market need emerges as the top reason, contributing to the downfall of 42% of startups[4]. In another analysis of 80 interviews with failed startup founders, only 10% cited competition as a problem, with just 2 out of 80 stating it was the main reason for failure[5]. The most prevalent fatal mistake? Building something people simply don't need, with 42% of companies attributing their demise to a lack of market demand[6]. While competition can indeed spell trouble for startups, it can often be mitigated through cooperation and collaboration. So, while facing competition is inevitable for startup ideas, keeping perspective and focusing on addressing market needs is crucial.

This doesn't mean that the startups should not be protected against their competitors because if not tackled wisely and efficiently, competition can sometimes lead to the failure of startups. Plants, too, have a unique mechanism to defend against their competition naturally. Through "Allelopathy," they can naturally produce chemicals that protect the plant from insect attack and microbial infection. Allelopathy is the production and release of a chemical by one organism that is either detrimental or beneficial to another organism[7]. For example, rice varieties (Oryza sativa) produce a compound known as momilactone B when growing near an agricultural weed called barnyard grass. Enzymes in allelopathic rice synthesize momilactones, which support the rice crop's success by suppressing the growth of barnyard grass and other weeds[8].

Furthermore, growing allelopathic varieties of other crops, like rice, can make the entire crop system less vulnerable to weed competition and pathogens. In 2006, during a talk at the StartUp School, Paul Graham, the Co-founder of Y Combinator, stated that competitors are not the biggest threat to any startup[9].

While competition poses a risk to startups, it's one of many potential pitfalls. Internal disputes, inertia, and perhaps ignoring users all can bring a startup crashing down. Of these, neglecting users is often the most perilous. Rather than solely focusing on defending against competitors, startups should prioritize understanding and addressing the needs of their customers. After all, if a startup fails to align with the desires of its target market, it's essentially offering a product or service that nobody wants. This issue becomes even more pronounced when a business introduces an innovative solution. In such cases, the risk of lacking market demand is significantly heightened. So, it is sometimes better to have competitors catering to the same target audience with similar offerings when launching an innovative product or service[10]. This ensures that, as a founder, there is a market for your innovation, and you are not engaged in a direct zero-sum game. Instead, your innovation becomes the key differentiator, allowing you to outshine existing players in the market.

However, if a startup founder intends to commence a business that is common, in that case, if there are big and direct competitors in the same place or market niche, then it is a bad sign because even though the lack of market needs risk is much lower, but the lack of differentiation would make it hard to wind over the already existing bigger competitors who are already offering the same solution better and in most cases, cheaper too.

Navigating competition requires avoiding two extremes. If no existing business offers what you intend to provide, it could signal a lack of market demand for your product or service. In this case, it's wise to validate and pilot-test your idea before launching on a large scale, saving you from investing resources into a potentially unsuccessful venture.

Conversely, if your startup aims to solve a problem already addressed by an existing business or large company, the key lies in differentiation. To stand out, your product or service must offer something unique. By incorporating distinctive features, you can create a unique selling proposition that appeals to a specific niche within a broader market segment.

For plants, competition for resources is considered a source of their stress, which also determines the distribution and evolution of the plant species[11]. Eugenius Warming (1909) observed that there are many plant species that could be found in a botanical garden when isolated from interacting with other plants, unlike those that could not maintain themselves when subjected to competition from other species[12]. Various factors could limit plant growth, but the three most important resources for which plants compete are nutrients, water, and sunlight. In the soil, where the nutrient concentration varies, the plants try to concentrate their roots to absorb more nutrients than their competitors. Similarly, in conditions where water availability is less in the soil, the plants try to showcase adaptations that reduce water loss from their leaves through transpiration. To deal with the light competition, either the plant shows movement based on the motion of the light, or it tries to grow unevenly such that there are larger parts grown in the areas where there are chances of more absorption of sunlight.

Like plants competing for resources in different environments, organizations also engage in diverse forms of competition. Throughout history, companies have sought to gain an edge over rivals through unique strategies through disruptive innovations[13]. In the 1960s, the focus was on efficiency, with companies striving to minimize the time, resources, and labor required for production. Those adept at this approach gained a competitive advantage. Another competitive factor was scale, which emphasized cost and pricing dynamics. However, in the early 1980s, there was a paradigm shift towards quality, spurred by W. Edwards Deming's advocacy for quality as a cornerstone of Japanese manufacturing. This led to focusing on product and service excellence through methodologies like Six Sigma quality control[14].

Today, competition revolves around quality, efficiency, and scale. While some companies, like Wal-Mart and Ford, compete primarily on pricing, others, such as Nordstrom and BMW, prioritize quality in their competitive strategies. This led to the emergence of the "Lean Six Sigma." Instead of separately looking at Six Sigma and lean production, companies began competing on reduced costs and better quality. Another repositioning of the competition came with the emergence of the internet during the 1990s, which made companies compete based on the number of people who use their products/services instead of calculating cost or quality (or both). In this race, Microsoft apparently became the first to compete based on the network as it developed its operating system to be compatible with any personal computer. Following their footsteps came Google, Facebook, LinkedIn, etc., which competed based on the network of people they could reach. However, the most recent way in which the companies currently compete is through the ecosystem. Competing by building an ecosystem refers to collaborating with or co-opting third parties to build a unique value proposition by leveraging specific products and services and combining them together so that they have more total utility for the customers. Thus, the focus has shifted from the number of customers served to the number of partners a company works with on top of its products and services.

The shifts in the parameters don't mean that the companies do not compete based on the other forces. There is always heightened use of one parameter over another in varying situations. For example, efficiency takes center stage when the economic situation is bad; scale becomes a strategic priority when there is decelerated growth in the industry; quality comes to the forefront when the growth in market trends is healthy, and networks and ecosystems come into the spotlight when differentiating a product or a service becomes too difficult as a way of producing an advantaged value proposition. Besides all these historical parameters of competing, companies could still compete based on several other grounds such as agility, the quicker the change and adaptation, the better market capture, or through disruption by completely reimagining certain conventional business models and even through data analytics by investing heavily in data and then driving greater efficiencies into their operations to produce better-tailored products, services, and unique experiences for their customers. No matter which strategy a company uses to compete with others, it cannot be the same for all. Just like unique products, the way companies compete is also different. Thus, you as an entrepreneur should not compete based on one strategy just because others are using it, instead, choose what strategy works best for you based on your unique circumstances and market needs.

COMPETITION DIVIDES, COLLABORATION MULTIPLIES

Now, let's explore the fascinating world of plants from a different perspective. While we often think of plants as competing with one another for essential resources like nutrients, sunlight, and water, they also have an incredible ability to form mutually beneficial relationships.

Beyond their interactions within the plant world, plants also establish symbiotic connections with species outside their plant world. Take, for instance, the *Nepenthes rajah*, a carnivorous pitcher plant found in nutrient-deficient hilly areas. This unique plant forms a symbiotic bond with a small mammal, a treeshrew, akin to a squirrel.

The *Nepenthes rajah* entices the treeshrew with sweet nectar, inviting it to visit and explore its jug-like leaves. In return, the treeshrew utilizes the pitcher plant as a convenient spot for biological needs, depositing nitrogen-rich feces into the pitcher.

Pitcher plants are known for their mechanism of trapping insects and other organisms that come on their surface by secreting chemicals that make them slip, causing the insects to lose their grip and eventually fall inside. But *Nepenthes rajah* grows in hilly areas which are nutrient deficient. So, instead of killing the available species population, it maintains a mutually beneficial relationship with them[15]. The Nepenthes pitcher plant doesn't have a slippery surface because its motive is not to eat but to attract the treeshrew. The way it does that is unique in itself. The pitcher plant has modified itself so that the top of the pitcher is like a toilet bowl lid. The lid angles upward over the top of the pitcher, and the nectar is on the edge of the lid. The distance from the nectar to the front of the pitcher's opening is the exact same length as the treeshrew. This forces the animal to straddle the rim as it licks the nectar off the lid, and its feces drop directly into the pitcher.

This simple yet captivating tale of plant-mammal symbiosis is a powerful reminder of the potential for collaboration and mutual benefit, even across seemingly disparate realms. It illustrates how, by forging symbiotic relationships with entities outside our immediate industry or domain, we can unlock remarkable opportunities for growth and innovation.

Just as the *Nepenthes rajah* and the treeshrew have found a way to meet their respective needs through collaboration, startups can also achieve remarkable feats by partnering with individuals and organizations from diverse backgrounds and industries. By embracing collaboration and fostering symbiotic relationships, we not only address our own needs but also contribute to the growth and success of others.

This story encourages us to think beyond traditional boundaries and explore the possibilities that emerge when we come together with a shared purpose. It reminds us that by embracing diversity and working collaboratively, we have the potential to create wonders and drive meaningful impact in our respective endeavors.

Competition is not immanently bad but sometimes holds us back from achieving the greatest potential, while collaboration allows us to progress not as separate entities but as a whole to achieve the benefit for all. This is shown by the plants that partner with or build relationships with other plants, mammals, and bacteria. For example, legume crops, such as peas, beans, etc., form a partnership with a specific type of bacteria called Rhizobium, and they together form a structure called Nodules[16]. These nodules act as a safe place for the bacteria to live, where they receive food from the plant in the form of sugars. In turn, this Rhizobium has the ability to convert the nitrogen gas in the atmosphere into ammonia, which is required by the plant for photosynthesis. In this way, the plant gets its required nutrients, and the bacteria gets its home and food, thus maintaining a cooperative relationship where both benefit.

In the intricate dance of nature, even plants rely on symbiotic partnerships to thrive, particularly in their early stages of growth. One such remarkable alliance exists between orchid plants and specific fungi, revealing the interdependence woven into the fabric of the natural world.

As orchid seedlings take their first step into the world, they rely entirely on mycorrhizal fungi for vital resources for their initial growth. These fungi, known as mycorrhizas, play a pivotal role in the orchid's journey, acting as indispensable allies in their quest for sustenance.

At the heart of this partnership lies a critical exchange: mycorrhizas assist orchids in uptaking a precious resource – phosphorus – that is notoriously difficult for plants to obtain. Bound tightly to soil particles, phosphorus presents a formidable challenge for young orchids seeking nourishment. Enter the mycorrhizas, extending a helping hand to bridge this gap, facilitating phosphorus absorption from the soil and empowering orchids to flourish. In this symbiotic dance of give and take, orchids and mycorrhizas exemplify the profound beauty and interconnectedness of the natural world, where mutual cooperation paves the way for growth and resilience.

In the book, "The Collaboration Imperative," by Ron Ricci and Carl Wiese, they clearly state why collaboration matters for every business and startups[17]. According to them, consensus leads to a win-lose and sometimes a lose-lose situation, but collaboration between organizations leads to a win-win situation. However, this collaborative mindset should be ingrained among all the employees and leadership at all levels. Instead of internal competition and bureaucracy, organizations should promote a culture of collaboration. Brilliant ideas can come from anywhere, so the more voices, the better the brainstorming. Collaboration enhances communication at all organizational levels, which is crucial for a company's growth. By collaborating internally and externally, organizations can create more value by allowing more perspectives to discuss and make decisions.

In today's highly competitive and unpredictable environment, doing one thing better than your competitors is not enough. You must adapt your organization to rapidly recognize and adapt to new opportunities and threats. Collaboration is the new imperative. It may be the only way to accelerate innovation, improve agility, increase adaptability, and cut costs all at once[18].

THE TALE OF THREE SISTERS

The Three Sisters Garden is a timeless example of the beauty of synergy among plants, showcasing how diverse species can harmonize and thrive together in a way that surpasses individual growth. The way different plants combine is an art that can be practiced such that they all complement each other by increasing the bloom, providing nutrients, or by their flowery scent.

Each plant plays a unique role in this botanical ballet, contributing its distinct strengths to the ensemble. Some plants may excel in bolstering bloom, while others provide essential nutrients or infuse the garden with their delightful scents. It's a choreography of cooperation where every plant finds its place and purpose, creating a symphony of beauty and abundance.

Take, for instance, the Italian honeysuckle, whose fragrant blooms perfume the evening air with their scent, filling the garden with a sense of serenity and allure. Meanwhile, with its fading fragrance, the rose gracefully yields the stage, allowing the honeysuckle's aroma to take center stage.

In the example of Three Sisters Garden, we witness an amazing magic that unfolds when different plants come together in perfect harmony, showcasing the boundless potential of collaboration and cooperation in nature's grand design.

Combining these two flowery plants in the garden can aromatize the whole day. The Three Sisters Garden is the term used for a plant combination that uniquely benefits each other by enhancing efficiency and productivity. The "Three Sisters" is the name given to the corn, beans, and squash plants, all grown simultaneously in the same field but through an intercropping system[19]. A typical garden of three sisters is structured so that the corn is planted at the center. The beans are planted around the corn in a ring-like pattern, and the squash is planted at the edges of the field. Corn is considered the oldest sister as she stands tall, right at the center. The corn is a natural pole for the bean vines to climb. Corn and bean vines combined together give shade to the squash. Squash is considered to be the second sister as by growing at the edges, it protects the other three sisters from weeds and also shades the soil. Beans are considered the third sister as the bean vines help stabilize the corn plants, protecting them from blowing over easily by the winds. Beans also help in keeping the soil fertile. Apart from mutually benefiting each other, these three sisters are also planted in a small area so that the entire space can be utilized contemplatively.

This unique symbiotic relationship between these three sisters allows them to produce more fruit, using less water and fertilizers[20]. Corn, beans, and squash complement each other in their growth process and provide a great combination of nutritional benefits to humans. While the dried beans are rich in protein, corn provides carbohydrates, and squash yields both vitamins from the fruit and healthy, delicious oil from the seeds.

Nevertheless, to achieve such a bountiful yield, all three sisters must be present together; the absence of any of them would not be sufficient for the optimal growth of the plants. All three must be present together to mutually benefit each other's growth.

For example, the bean vines would have nothing to climb on without corn. Similarly, the corn and the squash would not have enough nutrients without beans. Also, without the squash, the roots of the corn would run dry and eventually die as the squash leaves provide shade for the shallow roots of the corn.

Just as plants thrive when they collaborate harmoniously, organizations can reap tremendous benefits from fostering a culture of collaboration among their members. In large companies with sprawling teams, internal collaboration and continuous learning from senior leaders can lay the foundation for a vibrant culture of teamwork and innovation.

Take, for instance, the executives at Standard Chartered Bank, who serve as exemplary role models in cooperation. With a heritage rooted in global trading, the bank's leaders have honed their collaborative skills over time, setting a shining example for their colleagues[21]. Their commitment to collaboration extends beyond mere teamwork – it's about sharing knowledge, best practices, and insights gleaned from years of experience.

In today's dynamic business landscape, collaboration isn't just about working together; it's about cultivating a continuous learning and improvement culture. By embracing collaboration as a cornerstone value, organizations can unlock new levels of creativity, efficiency, and success, drawing inspiration from the harmonious interplay of nature's own collaborative masterpieces.

Partnerships and collaborations catalyze rapid organizational growth, enabling companies to scale up exponentially and drive innovation. A prime example of this is Reliance Industries Limited, a multinational conglomerate that has forged strategic alliances with various companies to accelerate the deployment of 5G technology in India.

These partnerships are instrumental in individual companies' growth and fueling economic development on a broader scale. By leveraging each other's strengths and resources, companies can create synergies that benefit both parties and customers.

Take, for instance, the collaboration between Reliance Jio and Meta on the metaverse, a shared virtual space where users can interact in real time[22]. This partnership exemplifies how companies can come together to explore new frontiers and shape the future of technology and connectivity.

In the ever-evolving business and technology landscape, partnerships are essential for progress and innovation. By fostering collaborative relationships, organizations can unlock new opportunities, drive growth, and create value for all stakeholders.

In addition, Reliance is also collaborating with Google on Cloud to manufacture incredibly affordable 5G cell phones and partnering with Microsoft and Intel to create world-class infrastructure, computing, and 5G edge computing[23]. In 2022, Reliance took a step ahead and collaborated with Qualcomm to develop a 5G solution for India, which can be expanded globally[24]. All these partnerships benefit these tech companies and MNCs to expand. There are indirect jobs that are derivatives of the original innovations. This creates a symbiotic relationship between different industries. Just the way one sapling or a tree might be dependent on fungi or algae for some of their nutrient requirements, in the same way, the entire travel industry depends upon the availability of cheap air and land travel. Destinations like the Eiffel Tower, Universal Studios, and Disney World would never have been economically viable if their customers couldn't travel and come from different parts of the world. Along the same lines, the retail and wholesale industries, in the present scenario, are completely dependent on the road/rail/air distribution system. Wal-Mart, the largest private sector employer in the country, built its business model around the effective use of information technology and sourcing cheap products[25].

As we forward, let's heed nature's wisdom and prioritize collaboration over competition, knowing that together, we can achieve far greater heights than we could ever imagine alone. Plants, when given the choice between competition and collaboration, opt for the latter to mutually enhance their growth. While healthy competition has its merits, collaboration ensures a win-win scenario for all involved. So, let's unlock the potential for exponential growth and a brighter collective future by embracing collaboration, sharing resources, and supporting one another.

You possess skills that I don't,

Will we compete? No, we won't!!

I can do things that you cannot.

Can we join hands? Of course, why not!!

– Amya Madan

8.

STABILITY & SUSTAINABILITY

THE CORNERSTONES OF A SOLID FOUNDATION

---

*"Sustainability is no longer about doing less harm.
It's about doing more good."*

– Jochen Zeitz

In the words of Paul Hawken, "The first rule of sustainability is to align with natural forces, or at least try not to defy them." Sustainability is at the core of the societal goal: to make planet Earth safe for humans to co-exist over a long time. For this reason, the 17 Sustainable Development Goals (SDGs) provide guidance or act as a rulebook for people worldwide to take action and look for solutions that address the global challenges facing the international community.

The unique designs in nature have always inspired innovators to look for solutions to some of the most striking challenges. Human beings have always been fascinated by underwater life. Like fishes swimming underwater, many people have attempted to dive deep into the waters to experience a completely new and different life. This is not only a source of pleasure and happiness for people but also a source of new and innovative ideas, learning from marine life.

One such unique design in nature inspired the Founder of Amphibio, Jun Kamei, in the United Kingdom[1]. How fishes stay and breathe underwater for so long with the help of their light-weighted gills, is no longer a mystery,. Nevertheless, how those gills can help humans breathe longer underwater is what this startup has been able to decode and achieve. Their artificial physical gills hold the potential to transform the way humans breathe underwater. This startup is constantly learning from the life underwater, their survival principles, and creating a space for human beings by translating those nature-inspired ideas into impactful innovations.

Another attempt is to create Amphitex™, a sustainable and 100% recyclable alternative to traditional waterproof breathable textiles, heavily used in outdoor apparel[1]. Due to human-activity-induced global warming and the melting of glaciers, there has been a rise in the sea water level. This problem made these founders rethink and reinvent the life of human beings, if not on land, then underwater. With a futuristic view in mind, they have redesigned how humankind might live due to the rising sea level, which would force them to live close to the water. Their solution also enables people to survive better in coastal cities with a constant flood threat and underwater submergence. Amphibio products are classic examples of how the entrepreneurial mindset can create innovative solutions for future generations by learning simple ways of doing things from nature. Their further expansion to newer products lies in creating Amphidry™ Yarn, a superhydrophobic yarn that converts into a chemical coating-free water resistant fabric[1]. Imagining a life underwater for humans enabled these innovators to design equipment that would easily make this possible much before we face the repercussions of our mismanaged behavior towards nature.

From water to wind, nature has provided us with everything. While startups like Amphibio were inspired by life underwater, others were inspired by the wind around them and converted it into a renewable energy source. Our planet needs more and better sources of renewable energy generation, and Biome Renewables[2], established in Canada, has come up as a rescue through its innovative product, the PowerCone®.

What inspired the creators of this wind turbine was that we cannot create more wind, but we can make the most of what is blowing[2]. The PowerCone is a turbine retrofit that channels incoming wind onto the blades to address root leakage. The result is not just more power, but power from a place where no bigger blade or more intelligent software can find it[2]. The major problem conventional wind turbines face is 'Root Leakage', which is at the core of what robs these wind turbines of power. This root leakage is responsible for generating turbulence by drawing power away from its blades. Nature also has a solution for this problem, depicted by how effectively a kingfisher and a maple seed move through the fluids. Taking lessons from the Maple seed, the PowerCone was born. Maple seeds have developed a unique mechanism of spinning like a tornado to disperse their seeds at a distance farther from where the tree is.

Scattering seeds or dispersal is a notable mechanism in all plants, often assisted by birds and wind[3]. However, by getting caught in a gust of wind, seeds tend to fall and grow close to one another. The maple seeds adapted a phenomenon to combat this problem. Twirling a tornado-like vortex, it created more lift than its non-twirling counterparts. This allows them to increase the seeds' reach and fall at a place farther than the tree.

Not just that, there is a difference in the distance traveled by a dead (brown-colored) seed compared to a alive (green-colored) seed. This is because there is an altered center of gravity in the brown-colored dead seeds, closer to the center of lift, similar to a paper airplane that can fly further than its opponents[3]. By carefully studying how maple seed spirals through the air, scientists were inspired to design the first smallest known monocopter. Continuing on the same path, Biome Renewables is unveiling the potential of this unique strategy of maple seeds by applying it to wind turbines to deal with turbulent air and increase the amount of renewable energy that can be extracted from the wind. The PowerCone attaches directly to the turbine's hub and rotates with the rotor, helping it capture more of the wind that's already blowing[2,3].

LET'S LEARN FROM NATURE TO MAKE IT SUSTAINABLE.

While we attempt to align businesses and startups according to the 17 sustainable goals, plants around us have already provided answers by showing stability backed by sustainability. By learning from these plants, startups can achieve both stability and sustainability.

To tackle the global hunger issues, the 2nd Sustainable Development Goal was established: Zero Hunger. 25% of the fruits and vegetables produced yearly are lost or wasted because of fungal spoilage[4]. However, in an attempt to prevent this loss, many farmers use synthetic fungicides, which can cause consequential harm to both humans and the environment.

Moreover, excessive use of fungicides can make fungi resistant over time. To avoid this, plants already have a unique natural mechanism to prevent the growth of fungi on their surface by developing anti-fungal compounds, thereby protecting themselves. These natural volatile molecules produced by plants protect them from many fungal diseases and stimulate other plants surrounding them to activate their defense systems.

Applying these principles of the plant to combat the issue of hunger, many startups have already begun their journey towards achieving SDG 2. Nanomik Biotechnology, taking inspiration from the plants, has abridged compounds similar to those released by the plants and has created a liquid fungicide that can be sprayed on crops in the field during and after harvest[5]. When a fungus tries to infect a fruit or vegetable by growing on its surface, it makes the pH of the plant surface more acidic. This makes the capsule containing the anti-fungal compounds break open, killing the fungus.

Thus, not only is there a reduced use of chemicals, but there is also a massive reduction in food wastage! Goal accomplished!

Did you know? Globally, 2.6 billion people lack safe toilet access[6]. Sustainable Development Goal 3 has been laid down to ensure healthy lives worldwide and promote well-being for all ages[7]. Most often, people who live in poor and vulnerable communities are the most affected by a lack of proper sanitation, which causes unhealthy environmental conditions around them and affects their overall health and well-being. Within the 40% of the world who lack proper access to sanitation, a more profound problem lies with women and girls. 20%-40% of girls drop out of school because of inaccessible or inappropriate toilets[6]. This situation further aggravates the relief camps where aid is available during a natural disaster, but there is no proper and safe sanitation. That is why UNESCO also laid down SDG 6, which is to ensure clean drinking water and safe sanitation. With the accomplishment of Goal 6, ensuring well-being and health for all can also be taken care of. According to the report by UNICEF and the World Health Organization (2019), billions worldwide continue to suffer from poor access to water, sanitation, and hygiene. Approximately 2.2 billion people worldwide do not have safely managed drinking water services, 4.2 billion people do not have safely managed sanitation services, and 3 billion lack basic handwashing facilities[8]. However, plants have an answer to these two problems as well; the only pre-requisite is to have an innovative, creative, and curious mind to be able to observe their phenomenon and, with the right entrepreneurial mindset, establish a startup that not only revolutionizes the industry but also builds a sustainable future.

Evapotranspiration (ET) is the answer to this problem being faced worldwide.

We all have studied the concept of evaporation, which occurs at the surface of a liquid and converts into a gaseous state.

Similarly, transpiration is the process by which water evaporates from the surface of leaves into the atmosphere. A typical plant, found across any demography, absorbs water from the soil through its roots. Through osmosis (movement of water from one part to another), this water enters the plant and performs various metabolic and physiological functions. It travels across the plant system and then, eventually, is released into the atmosphere in the form of vapor via the plant's stomata, which are tiny, porelike structures on the surfaces of leaves that open or close to allow water to evaporate. The entire process of water uptake by the roots, water transportation through plant tissues, and finally, the release of the vapor by leaves into the atmosphere is known as transpiration. There are other instances when water evaporates directly into the atmosphere from soil near the plant. Together, this phenomenon is called well evapotranspiration (ET). By observing this process, startups have tried replicating this phenomenon to tackle the sanitation problem. change:WATER Labs have taken an elemental step towards developing a low-cost, compact, waterless toilet for non-sewered households and communities, inspired by the process of evapotranspiration in plants[9]. Their novel way of disposing of human waste is by allowing the water to evaporate. They have developed low-cost, portable toilets that use a simple membrane to evaporate 95% of sewage without any energy rapidly. Thus, working toilets can be built in rural villages and communities without the need for power or plumbing. The compact, contained, independent units can be dropped into any space quickly, and the 'self-flushing' technology works while being completely waterless and environmentally safe[10].

To ultimately achieve SDG 6, ensuring clean drinking is also vital. Following a keen observation, an entrepreneurial mindset, and lessons from plants, SolAqua developed The Rainmaker™ 330, a solar still that collects rainwater and transforms it into clean drinking water[11]. By employing the process of natural evaporation in plants and condensation, this device allows for natural pH buffering that produces clean, excellent-tasting water compared to steam distillation. With such innovations happening around the globe, we will be able to achieve the entire list of sustainable development goals very soon; most of them, taking inspiration from the plants and natural ecosystems around us.

"Build resilient infrastructure, promote inclusive and sustainable industrialization and foster innovation," says the Sustainable Development Goal 9. At the same time, we are learning from plants how to ensure stability and sustainability in organizations. While growing startups, there is much to learn from them by building infrastructure that fosters innovation and promotes inclusivity and sustainability.

Exemplifying the unique properties of sycamore maple seedpods here again can help achieve SDG 9 of building marvels through its distinctive nature. The sycamore maple is a large, spreading, broadleaf tree growing 115 feet tall and has a deep, branched root system that provides stability against strong winds. Nevertheless, maple trees aren't just good at resisting the wind but also ingenious in using it[12]. The seeds produced by the maple tree are winged and have a unique capability to spin as they fall. That is also why some call them helicopter seeds or samaras. The maple tree seedpods and several other plants have evolved similarly behaving seeds over the years. No matter how the seeds appear while attached to the tree, they quickly self-orient themselves and begin auto-rotating as soon as they detach from the tree. This allows the seed to slow down its process of falling, thereby getting enough time and chance to be carried away by the wind and passing breeze.

Are you wondering how they orient themselves and start spinning independently? Well, this is their exclusive act of balancing. Usually, the head of the seed has a weight more than the wing of the seeds. However, the seed's wings are much broader, allowing them to catch more air while falling. When the seed detaches itself from the tree, its head bends downward and advances compared to the wings. When the broadest part of the wing comes in contact with the wind, it slows down due to air resistance, forcing it to tilt with respect to the ground. As air rushes upward, encountering the tilted wing, it causes a deflection in the angle of the seed, resulting in the wing of the seed getting pushed in the opposite direction. However, while only the wings are deflected, the falling seed head, encountering little air resistance over its compact body, maintains its composure and descends linearly. The seed head works like an axle around which the wings are seen spinning. While gravity continues to act and lets the seed fall, the rotating wing keeps resisting its quick descent on the ground, keeping the doors of opportunity open for the winds passing by to drift the seed on an oblique journey, spreading it far away from the mother tree.

Startups are poised to revolutionize various industries with innovative ideas by taking inspiration from nature's simple yet ingenious designs.

Take, for instance, the Sycamore Ceiling Fan, which has reimagined the conventional ceiling fan by mimicking the structure of a falling Sycamore tree seed pod[13]. Unlike traditional fans with flat blades, the Sycamore Ceiling Fan boasts curved blades that emulate the efficient airflow of maple seeds. This unique design allows the fan to operate smoothly at low speeds while delivering powerful airflow with minimal turbulence and noise. By harnessing the natural principles of balance and efficiency, this fan offers a cost-effective and energy-efficient alternative to traditional ceiling fans, paving the way for sustainable and eco-friendly solutions in the infrastructure sector.

Isn't it incredible! We have successfully achieved many sustainable development goals by taking inspiration from the plants! Well! That is the beauty of nature. But sustainability isn't enough. Organizations and startups should also remain stable over the years to emerge victorious.

Recently added to the list is the 17th Sustainable Development Goal, which is all about building and nurturing partnerships across industries to build a stable and sustainable economy. Diversity in nature provides another classic lesson of how partnerships help maintain stability over time.

While we have discussed the lessons from rainforests, we can find valuable insights from the Prairie grasslands, where many flora species interact and collaborate to maintain a harmonious and resilient environment.

In a thriving ecosystem, diversity is key to stability and health. Rather than relying on a single species to fulfill specific functions, Prairie grasslands demonstrate the importance of having multiple species serving similar roles. For instance, instead of one type of organism solely responsible for soil fertilization or predator population control, a variety of species contribute to these essential ecological tasks, ensuring a balanced and sustainable ecosystem. This diversity enhances resilience and fosters a dynamic and interconnected web of life, highlighting the significance of collaboration and mutual support in nature's intricate tapestry. This redundancy builds better resilience and stability in the ecosystem and supports various natural organisms. It also protects from natural disturbances like fires, disease, or calamity. The redundancy of functions ensures that due to unprecedented conditions, if one entire species becomes extinct or can't survive the ravages of time, another species with a similar role can serve and react to the changing stimuli in a better manner to thrive after the disturbance, ensuring that the ecosystem remains resilient.

Consider a situation in which a prairie grassland ecosystem's main food-producing plant gets wrecked by fire[14]. In that instance, hitherto, another plant species that was less abundant may now get better suited to live in the new soil conditions and, therefore can become the new dominant food-producing plant species serving the grassland. However, this could be possible as long as the post-fire composition of plant species fills the void by performing the same functional role as the pre-fire plant community.

Only then can we call the prairie stable, as it will be able to survive the fire intact.

Drawing Parallels Between a Tree Trunk and the Stability of a Startup

Not just the ecosystem as a whole, but the parts of a plant also provide stability, which is analogous to what organizations and startups require to thrive in difficult situations. The tree trunk is analogous to the stability startups seek in their overall structure and functioning. Have you ever seen a tree without a trunk? Unless it is an alien. None of us have seen a big tree without a trunk. The trunk of a tree is the most dominant part, providing stability and an identity. All the branches, leaves, fruits, and flowers cannot grow unless a trunk supports them all single-handedly. The roots can also be of no effect if they are not attached to the base of a tree trunk. The vitality of a trunk is because of its role for a tree, which is to provide it with immense strength, support, and protection, and not only that but also to let the tree grow and thrive.

Understanding the structure of a tree trunk is a key to unlocking how trees can be so valuable. This trunk is responsible for connecting the leafy crown with the roots down in the soil, and while the roots perform a vital role in absorbing water from the soil, the trunk is where the core system prevails, enabling the water and nutrients to reach the tip of the leaves. Not just that, pluck a flower, fruit, or leaf from the tree, and you will be able to do it without any effort, but try cutting the tree trunk, and you will know what strength it is.

At the core of every successful organization lies its leadership, similar to the sturdy trunk of a tree providing stability and resilience. Without agile leadership steering the way, an organization's growth and prosperity are but distant dreams. Agile leadership acts as the anchor, adept at navigating through obstacles and transforming challenges into opportunities for growth. Just as a tree's trunk withstands the forces of nature, from fierce winds to scorching heat, effective leadership guides the organization through turbulent times, ensuring the well-being and productivity of its members. Much like the indispensable role of a trunk in supporting the tree's canopy, strong leadership is essential for fostering a thriving and resilient organizational culture.

No tree has the good fortune of not encountering any storm, thunder, or harsh weather conditions during its lifetime, just as no business remains unaffected by the uncertainty of global markets, industrial regulations, or politics. However, to provide strength to the people and to lead them successfully under turbulent and stressful conditions, requires leadership that provides strength in the form of physical stability and psychological security.

Is it important? Indeed, it is! Competition can easily break a fragile startup both internally and externally. Stability in terms of physical strength would ensure that the people in an organization are physically safe because of the available tools and resources needed to work safely and effectively[15]. At the same time, it is equally important to ensure psychological security. This can be achieved by building mutual trust between the leaders and the employees and aligning the company's vision so that they seek the organization's future as a symbol of their accomplishments.

Have you ever observed what happens when you damage the base of a tree trunk? Gradually, the entire trunk becomes weak, developing cracks and decay. This deterioration can ultimately lead to the tree's collapse.

Similarly, when an organization's leadership fails to prioritize its employees' well-being, the consequences can be equally dire. Even a single disruption can unsettle employees, impairing their focus, adaptability, and overall performance. For instance, discussions about a potential merger can breed uncertainty among employees, eroding their commitment and fueling job insecurities. This uncertainty acts like decay, undermining individuals' and teams' ability to stay engaged and dedicated.

Consequently, the company's growth suffers as productivity declines. Regardless of the cause, effective leadership, like the tree trunk, must shield employees against instability and ensure organizational stability. The pine trees have a unique mechanism to withstand wind and snow. Instead of straight-grained materials, their trunk is made up of spiral-grained materials. This spiral composition helps protect trees that grow in high-wind areas from breaking[16]. This can be achieved due to an increased ability of the tree to bend and twist in solid winds, which reduces drag forces, allowing it to withstand additional weight (such as that from snow) by sliding it off from its branches when they twist in the wind.

The leadership in an organization should also adopt strategies that ensure that they twist and bend to maintain stability. The leadership should ensure that they provide the people in their organization with the right resources (a strong foundation) while periodically communicating the growth prospects, visions, and the company's progress coherently. By often checking on individual performance, the cracks within an organization can be avoided, and the void can be filled to ensure that it remains stable over time. This filling of gaps can sometimes be done with doses of motivation and optimism to keep all the functions in an organization aligned and committed.

Also, the organizations should ensure that their branches grow only as much as they can sustain without breaking. As observed by Leonardo da Vinci, a tree almost always grows so that the total thickness of the branches at a particular height is equal to the thickness of the trunk[17]. In the same fashion, an organization should also ensure that it branches out and diversifies, keeping in mind the original strength of its leadership to avoid breaking off.

Heavy rains pour, and strong winds blow.

Try breaking my trunk; my strength, I will show!

Be flexible enough to maintain agility,

But sustainable enough to ensure stability.

– Amya Madan

9.

PESTICIDES & PATENTS

SAFEGUARDING GROWTH

Inventions cannot be judged by patent parameters, but patents have the ability to take inventions very far.

– Kalyan C Kankanala

As a growing sapling requires essential nutrients, water, and fertilizers for healthy development, it also needs protection from pests and diseases. Without adequate pest control measures, crops face a constant threat of infestation, which can destroy entire harvests. Despite the farmer's meticulous efforts to nurture the crops with optimal conditions and care, a single pest attack can spell disaster, rendering the crop unfit for consumption. In essence, once pests invade, the crop no longer belongs to the farmer—it becomes prey to the pests' voracious appetite, jeopardizing both yield and quality.

But why are we talking about pest attacks?

The crop results from a farmer's efforts, creativity, and innovation to produce the best. However, suddenly, some pests come and take over the crop erstwhile that belonged to them, making it their food now. *What will they do in such a situation?*

Had they sprayed pesticides before the attack, the pests would have been deterred from attacking the crop. Neither the plants had a natural mechanism to withstand pests, nor did a farmer provide them with protection using pesticides. Simple, the pests are bound to acquire a good and healthy crop.

In the entrepreneurship journey, where creativity, innovation, and hard work culminate in groundbreaking solutions, entrepreneurs invest years of dedication to nurture their ideas into impactful innovations. Just as farmers meticulously tend to their crops, entrepreneurs provide their creations with essential nutrients like mentorship and the financial fertilizers of angel funding, ensuring their growth and development. However, amidst the hustle of product development, one critical aspect often overlooked is safeguarding Intellectual Property Rights (IPR). It's similar to a farmer forgetting to protect their crop from pests.

The repercussions of neglecting IPR can be dire. Without proper patents or copyrights, entrepreneurs leave their innovations vulnerable to exploitation by competitors. Just as a farmer's crop falls prey to pests, competitors can swoop in, replicate the technology, and claim it as their own, eroding the entrepreneur's hard-earned market share.

Without legal protection, the entrepreneur cannot defend their innovation, helplessly watching as competitors seize control, the way farmers lose a crop to pest infestation.

This is not an atypical incidence but a regular phenomenon that can occur in both – the agricultural field and the startup world. Thus, farmers need to protect their crops from pest attacks by using pesticides. Entrepreneurs must also protect their innovation, invention, or product/service by filing for Intellectual Property Rights.

PESTS KEPT IN CHECK

There are about 30,000 species of weeds, 3,000 species of worms, and 10,000 species of plant-eating insects[1]. A farmer has to protect his crops from the attack of all these threats. Not only that, but a farmer also has to protect his crops even after they leave the field because pests can also attack them during storage or transportation. Thus, to ensure that the crops reach the consumers without getting attacked by pests, a farmer sprays pesticides in the right amount to make the plants pest-resistant.

Nearly 20% of crop production is lost to insects every year[2]. While the whole world is facing the challenge of hunger, food protection is crucial to prevent that. Farmers should be enlightened enough to reduce the percentage of wastage due to pest attacks and learn to use the most effective pesticides at the right time and in the right amount. More than half of the crops would be lost to pests and diseases without pesticides. Between 26 and 40 percent of the world's potential crop production is lost annually because of weeds, pests, and diseases[3]. Thus, crop protection is integral for farmers to produce more food on less land by protecting the plants from pesticide pest attacks. A study conducted by the U.S. estimated that without fungicides, yields of most fruits and vegetables would fall by 50-90 percent[4]. Suppose a farmer wishes to earn more profits. In that case, it is vital to protect the crops from pests, diseases, and weeds, which have the power to shatter the entire yield using pesticides

The use of pesticides, thus, benefits the farmers by protecting them from diseases, pests, and weeds and also increases the productivity of the soil, allowing the crops to continue growing. Using pesticides keeps specific threats at bay by creating a shield around the plants, allowing fresh plants to grow. Pesticides also ward off pests such as rats, mice, ticks, and mosquitoes while protecting them from microbial pests or weeds.

For example, rats can destroy crops by spreading bubonic plague, mosquitoes can spread malaria, and fleas can spread typhus[5]. The pesticides protect the crops from several diseases by averting all these pests. Does a farmer let the plants die unprotected? Of course not. Doing so would not only have repercussions for the farmer, in terms of loss of money and time, but can also have a catastrophic impact on the world, as the world will lose much of its food production, leaving innumerable people hungry.

WE ARE DEPENDENT ON PLANTS; THEY ARE NOT!

Since humans can be unpredictable, nature has its way of protecting itself from pests and diseases. Over the years, plants have evolved to protect themselves from the damage caused by pests and weeds. Several plants defend themselves either through morphological or physiological modifications. Researchers are studying plants' natural pest and disease resistance phenomenon to replicate it artificially and create natural and less harmful pesticides.

Morphologically, plants brace themselves by either changing the color of their leaves and flowers or altering the thickness of the cell walls and plant tissues, and sometimes by secreting a waxy surface coating or producing spines. These changes in the plant's overall appearance are done so that they become visually unimpressive to the insect, creating a physical barrier.

Drs. Maxwell and Jennings conducted a study to understand the economics of escape behavior in 13 pea varieties[6]. They found that the pea aphid, the small sap-sucking insect, preferred yellow-green plants to the dark-green ones because the dark green leaves are less attractive than the yellowing plants when under stress. Another example of this morphological adaptation in plants for pest resistance is seen in a variety of Brussels sprouts called "Rubine[7] ". This variety of Brussels plants has transformed the color of their foliage to red because the red foliage is less attractive to the cabbage worm than the green varieties.

Plants have a clever trick up their sleeves to fend off pests: they produce a thin layer of wax on their leaves and stems, which acts like a protective shield, keeping water inside the plant and releasing chemicals that bugs don't like. For example, raspberry plants secrete an acidic substance that beetles find unappealing, helping to keep them away and protect the plant from harm. It's like the plant's own built-in bug repellent!

Certain plants have a fascinating defense mechanism against insects: they produce microscopic hooked hair called trichomes, which serve as a barrier against hungry insects, making it difficult for them to feed. This natural adaptation is particularly common in plants growing in their native habitats. For instance, African violets develop such protective hair on their surface, effectively warding off insect attacks. Similarly, hollies have altered their leaf edges into spiny edges, which helps them keep the larvae of foliage-feeding moths from devouring whole leaves after eating only the spiny edges[7].

Would the absence of a farmer lead to the demise of all plant life due to the absence of protection against pests and diseases? Surprisingly, despite lacking human intervention, rainforests have thrived for centuries and generations.

Does that mean there is something that is protecting these plants from weeds, pests, insects, and diseases naturally? But what is it?

In scientific language, these are the "secondary metabolites," unique plant compounds that protect the plants naturally by providing them with a physiological defense mechanism. About 30,000 such secondary metabolites are known to researchers to date[7]. Plants, through their unique modifications and adaptation, have produced toxic chemicals that ward off pests and insects without causing any harm to their health. Researchers have tried to study these biologically produced insecticides and pesticides and artificially manufactured them to protect several plant varieties. Some plants, especially conifers, have also physiologically modified themselves to produce resin, a sticky substance, to dissuade bark beetles and borers from harming them[8].

As we advance with new technology and innovation, these natural ways of protecting plants can benefit farmers and create a safer planet by minimizing the use of chemical pesticides.

INTELLECTUAL PROPERTY RIGHTS – KEEPING INNOVATIONS PROTECTED

If a farmer can understand the importance of protecting his crop, for budding entrepreneurs, it is crucial to recognize the significance of protecting their creation, innovation, and startup. Intellectual Property (IP) encompasses various rights like copyrights, trademarks, and patents[9]. Securing these rights for any innovative product, service, and process in the early stages can safeguard their startup's growth. It is like a seed most vulnerable to pest attack during the sapling phase because of its delicacy. While startups are beginning their growth in the market, the innovations become more visible to people, and thus, the threat of infringement increases 10x times. That is why it is better to protect the innovation by patenting or copyrighting the product/service.

Protection using Intellectual Property Rights (IPR) acts as a shield that puts a legal check on the competition faced by the startups by preventing others from infringing the innovation, selling it in their name, or making profits through ther property. A patent for an innovation or a startup acts like the natural physiological adaptation in a plant, which protects it from several threats. A solid IP strategy provides protection against competitors and can serve as a magnet for investors, suppliers, partners, and other stakeholders. It's like having a shield that safeguards the original ideas and innovations while drawing in potential supporters and collaborators.

Each species has unique defense mechanisms to protect various parts of its structure in the plant kingdom. For instance, some plants arm their leaves with spiny edges, while others coat their outer layer with waxy substances to shield their delicate cuticles.

Additionally, certain plants deploy chemical compounds secreted from their roots to protect against threats. These diverse strategies highlight nature's ingenuity in safeguarding its plants from harm.

Just like plants have different mechanisms to protect various parts of their structure, startups need to safeguard different aspects of their identity. Whether it's their logo, name, color scheme, or innovative ideas, each element plays a vital role in defining the startup's uniqueness.

Like plants prioritize protection based on what is essential for their survival, startups must prioritize safeguarding the most significant aspects for their growth and success.

Pesticides, whether synthetic or natural, can aid in protecting a full-fledged yield of crops from getting destroyed and eaten up.

Similarly, good governance and IPR are crucial for the protection of innovation or startups from getting destroyed at the hands of competitors. A novel and innovative idea is the seed that blooms into a startup. An innovative idea, analogous to a seed, has the potential to grow into a successful startup worth millions. However, once these startups flourish, they become vulnerable to various threats, including idea theft, imitation of technology, and even unauthorized selling of the idea under a different name. Intellectual property laws are designed to protect these novel ideas, which are the cornerstone of a startup, and preserve the creative endeavors of entrepreneurs. Therefore, obtaining IP rights for a startup is a valuable asset, enhancing the commercial value of its innovations and providing a competitive edge in the market.

The farmer, aware that their crop secretes a protective chemical against pests, would hesitate to invest in a pesticide containing the same compound because such a purchase would only add unnecessary financial strain on him. However, determining whether a purchased pesticide mirrors the plant's natural defense requires expertise beyond the farmer's scope. Thus, the farmer could benefit from the assistance of a researcher or agricultural scientist proficient in this area, potentially saving substantial pesticide expenses. That is a scenario that an entrepreneur could face while filing a patent for his/her innovation or startup. Safeguarding startups from infringement demands more than mere protection—it necessitates a proactive search for existing Intellectual Property (IP) Rights held by other companies. It's like adding extra protection to a plant with natural defenses against pests. As startups grow, it's crucial to determine if other companies have patents, copyrights, or trademarks for the same ideas, products, colors, or logos that you, as an entrepreneur, want to protect. These initial steps can help avoid legal problems, like hefty fines for using someone else's ideas, and reduce the chances of lawsuits.

By filing for IP rights, a startup publicly announces, "Hey! This is my innovation. I own all the rights to it. And you have no right to copy, steal or sell it." Announcing this is essential as it deters competitors planning to imitate your innovation by warning them of the legal repercussions it might have on them. Successfully gaining rights over your startup in the form of a copyright, a patent, or any other type of IP empowers you to sue a company attempting to infringe your idea easily. Patenting the technology is particularly vital for tech startups, as IP protection gives them an edge over competitors and makes them more attractive to investors. Timing is also key—it's not just about filing for a patent but doing so at the right moment. Otherwise, all your hard work could go to waste if someone else files for a patent for the same innovation before you. Sometimes, IP can also be an additional source of income for startups as entrepreneurs can make money either from licensing, selling products, or transferring those rights to other conglomerates. For example, if an entrepreneur has a patent for a specific innovation, such as converting used chalk powder into a fresh chalk stick, but does not have the required resources to manufacture or commercialize it on a large scale, then by licensing or selling this innovation, he can earn revenue.

Conversely, without copyright, anyone can freely replicate his work and present it as their own without compensating him.

As startup founders meticulously craft strategies for various aspects of their ventures—like go-to-market approaches, business models, revenue streams, and target demographics—it's equally crucial to devise a plan for Intellectual Property (IP) protection. Neglecting to shield the intangible assets can be more costly to the company than a flawed marketing strategy. Entrepreneurs should outline a robust IP plan detailing what assets they intend to patent, how to draft patent applications effectively, when to file patents, and how to protect their startup from potential IP lawsuits.

GOOD GOVERNANCE - AN IMPERATIVE, NOT A CHOICE

Companies flourish not only due to the contributions of their employees and the support of their customers but also through effective corporate governance. A well-structured governance framework ensures that all stakeholders benefit from a harmonious work environment, from employees to customers and beyond. In such an environment, leaders with diverse skill sets seamlessly integrate with the company's workforce, teams, and stakeholders, fostering collaboration and driving collective success.

According to a report by Invest India, India has emerged as the 3rd largest ecosystem for startups with an overall tally of startup unicorns in India being 113[10]. Good governance is crucial for startups as it provides them with a structural framework and guides the operations and functioning of all the stakeholders, such as the employees, leadership, management, customers, the government, and other institutional and legal bodies. The framework constructed by good governance can influence the success of a startup, and therefore, it should be built on the foundations of integrity, ethics, and honesty. If a startup is a physical body, corporate governance can be its soul as it defines the company's morals, ethics, principles, and values, further guiding the behavior and overall conduct of the people connected with the startup.

In the absence of pesticides or natural pest resistance in plants, farmers use neem leaves or turmeric and spray it all over the plants to provide protection; good governance functions the same way. It is a hidden solution to the overall protection of a startup. According to the Confederation of Indian Industry (CII), "Corporate Governance deals with laws, procedures, practices and implicit rules that determine the power of the organization to form managerial decisions vis à-vis its claimants – especially, its shareholders, creditors, customers, the State and employees[11]." With experience, startup founders realized that running a business is not just about making profits or increasing valuation; heaps of other things are disguised behind the brand name and the company's market position. One such shroud force is corporate governance.

With the company's growth, scrutiny also grows, and good governance is crucial to protect the company from potential threats.

Corporate governance requirements can vary depending on the stage and size of a startup. However, founders should always prioritize Integrity, Transparency, and Accountability (ITAR) throughout all stages of governance.

In the early stages, incorporation assistance is needed when a startup starts or launches a product. As the startup grows, builds a team, gains traction, and earns revenue from customers, additional governance requirements such as GST registration, compliance with labor laws, and adherence to SEBI regulations become essential.

Financial considerations become paramount as the startup progresses to the expansion phase and seeks investments from venture capitalists and angel investors. This includes choosing suitable financial instruments, negotiating term sheets, and understanding valuation principles.

Continuous vigilance is crucial to prevent malpractices like bribery, employee harassment, or money laundering within the startup. While corporate governance may not be an everyday task for founders, it is vital for long-term success. Any delays or oversights in registration or tax filing can lead to penalties and financial burdens.

Effective governance ensures that startups navigate legal and corporate challenges smoothly, avoiding potential pitfalls during the entrepreneurial journey.

Thus, as an entrepreneur, while establishing the company's foundations, corporate governance should also be given due importance, which includes creating a cluster of rules, norms, and values that would guide the company's overall functioning internally, managed by the Board of Directors. Similar to how pesticides shield plants from harmful invaders, by integrating robust governance frameworks and securing IP rights, startups can foster a healthy environment for growth and innovation, ensuring sustainability and success in the dynamic business landscape.

Though tiny and wee,

crops can be destroyed by me.

Want to protect your hard work and innovation?

IPR is the way you can completely own your creation.

– Amya Madan

10.

INSIGHT & FORESIGHT

THE SECRETS OF PLANTS' STIMULATORY RESPONSES

The lush green freshness in you will always stay

Because you don't have wings to fly away,

But my one touch makes you shy away.

*H*ave you ever had the curious experience of touching a "Touch-me-not plant", also known as the *Mimosa pudica* plant? Perhaps you've marveled at how its leaves instantly fold up when touched as if the plant is retreating.

But have you ever wondered why it reacts in such a unique manner? What sets it apart from other plants that remain unaffected by touch?

Mimosa pudica is a sensitive plant that folds its leaves and droops its stems whenever touched by any other organism. Its rapid folding behavior protects it from the herbivores who get dissuaded by considering it very small. This enables the plant to survive despite threats from the environment. The Mimosa also exhibits a similar movement at night and when exposed to abiotic factors such as excessive heat and rain, protecting the plant from physical damage or desiccation (becoming completely dry)[1].

THE SCIENCE BEHIND STIMULATORY RESPONSES

Certain plants have developed remarkable mechanisms to adapt to their surroundings and respond swiftly to stimuli. This adaptation helps them thrive in changing environments and protects against threats. Take, for instance, the Mimosa plant's unique response to stimuli like touch. This reaction occurs because of a change in its turgor pressure, which is the pressure exerted by the water inside the plant cells against the cell walls.

With much water pushing against the cell wall, the turgor pressure is high, and the cell remains rigid. As and when the water moves out of the cell, there is a decrease in its turgor pressure, and the cell becomes flaccid. This movement of water in and out of the cell, called osmosis, occurs because of an unequal concentration of sodium and potassium ions on two sides of the membrane.

When an organism touches the surface of the leaflets of the Mimosa plant, the concentration gradient of potassium and chloride ions changes. This change in the potassium and chloride ions concentration is responsible for flowing the water out of the cells, making them flaccid, folding the leaflets, and drooping the midrib.

HARNESSING NATURE'S ADAPTIVE STRATEGIES FOR BUSINESS SUCCESS IN A VUCA WORLD

Carefully observing this unique plant phenomenon can inspire businesses and startups to respond effectively to their competition and the changes happening in the VUCA world. VUCA is no longer an adage. It has become a thought process, a perspective, and a way of approaching solutions to the diverse and dynamic problems of the ever-changing world. VUCA is an acronym for Volatility, Uncertainty, Complexity, and Ambiguity.

The current world is *'volatile,'* characterized by rapid and unpredictable changes occurring in our environment, making stability a rare commodity. Unlike the changes that have occurred in the past, the changes happening in today's world are more drastic, colossal, and unpredictable and are ensuing much faster. The world's growing *'uncertainty'* is due to a loosening connection with historical events and predictions, making it increasingly difficult to anticipate what comes next. Not knowing which disruption might come next has posed an issue for businesses when planning investment, growth, and development. The distinctive layers and boundaries have blurred, creating an intermingling of different layers, which adds to the world's *'complexity,'* making it challenging to recapitulate how things are interconnected. All choices seem tangled, one inside the other, creating a mesh of conditions and situations that do not have a single resolution strategy. The world has stopped following the "one size fits all" principles and has transitioned to a customized, specialized solution to every problem. With the *'ambiguity'* covering the entire landscape, not everything is black or white, not even grey, but now everything is colorful with its unique colors and shades. No more businesses are focusing on "what needs to be achieved"; they are more concerned about "why and how they need to achieve a goal," passing through a series of contradictions, conflicts, negotiations, and challenges. There is more acceptance for failing, learning, and then rising again to succeed.

However, for all the VUCA challenges in the VUCA world, there needs to be a **VUCA** solution or **VUCA mindset**. Just like a Mimosa plant immediately reacts to the changes around it, entrepreneurs and leaders also need to develop a VUCA mechanism to respond to the changing stimuli in their world.

This VUCA mechanism stands for

V- Veracity,

U- Understanding,

C- Creativity,

A- Agile Adaptability.

Especially in this growing world of the digital economy, organizations should possess **veracity** to access accurate and truthful data. Moreover, to ensure that the veracity of data is protected, it is crucial to secure that data against cyberattacks through proactive and industry-relevant threat intelligence.

Data veracity is indispensable because accurate data drives significant business decisions, allowing organizations to plan their next step strategically. The immense volume of data that it can process quickly outstrips the human mind's capacity. We no longer have the time or the ability to check everything personally or to trust our experience and instincts. Information has outpaced our ability to internalize and evaluate it[2]. As the digital revolution strides, there is a surge of entrusting decision-making processes to machine learning and artificial intelligence, which further exhibits the importance of data veracity coherently. AI and ML can make decisions based on their understanding of the information and data, which increases their dependency on the accuracy and truthfulness of the information. Even an imperceptible data manipulation can create havoc, potentially eroding public trust in the digital economy.

The concept of **understanding** in the VUCA mechanism broadens diverse horizons and perspectives. Organizations need to clearly understand their vision and goals to combat the uncertainty of this growing world, have an empathetic understanding of their target market, and have an in-depth understanding of their market trends. When these three elements of understanding are combined effectively, a business or a novel startup can grow its roots and deal with uncertain changes in the world. Understanding the customer's journey, their pain points, and their needs and diving deep into their real lives enables businesses to align their solutions better with the customers' problems and challenges. According to the Harvard Business Review, empathy is the most valuable and vital thing entrepreneurs and start-ups should learn[3]. James Allworth in Harvard Business Review writes that both Akio Morita of Sony and Steve Jobs were famous for never commissioning market research. Instead, they would just walk around the world watching what people did. They'd put themselves in the shoes of their customers[4]. Empathetic understanding of the customers allows organizations to provide better customer service and satisfaction.

Don't get perplexed by reading the word **creativity** in the VUCA mechanism. It indeed is the need of the hour – to deal with complex problems that prevail around us through creative thinking. Creativity has been at the core of the business for years but not much acknowledged as the top management agenda. Creativity, as we all know, is the skill to create something novel or out-of-the-box. All these years, we have not been able to measure or quantify creativity in tangible terms, which makes it elusive and thus less focused upon by organizations. However, there has been a shift in the world, which now focuses on more innovation-driven economic growth. The world now needs entrepreneurs and leaders who have shifted towards the right brains, and instead of following conventions, they are creatively looking for solutions. Zappos CEO highlighted that this creativity differentiates entrepreneurial thinking from the more traditional reasoning[5].

Ever wondered how mangrove tree seedlings survive despite relentless heavy water tides and without being swayed away by the strong winds?

The secret lies in their unique adaptation: germinating while still attached to their parent tree[6]. This unique adaptability feature shields the seeds from being swept away, allowing them to take root and grow into resilient trees. Doesn't this sound like the fourth VUCA mechanism of possessing agile adaptability?

In today's rapidly evolving landscape, organizations must not merely react to ambiguity; they must exhibit **agile adaptability** by swiftly adjusting to changing circumstances. Organizations ought to implement solutions in real-time as threats arise and maintain a flexible framework to navigate external shifts and internal conflicts without disrupting overall operations. Also, they should ensure an adaptable mechanism that the company constantly follows so that any change in the external environment or internal conflicts, doesn't harm the organization's overall functioning. As mangrove seeds thrive amidst adversity, businesses can flourish by embracing agile adaptability as a core principle of resilience and growth.

DEVELOPING INSIGHT AND FORESIGHT IN ORGANIZATIONS

Plants possess a unique characteristic feature of using a Hypersensitive Response (HR) system. When a plant is attacked, this system kicks into gear, performing gene-for-gene recognition and triggering a rapid response. This quick reaction leads to the rapid death of cells around the site of attack[7]. As a result, the damaged tissue is detached, preventing pathogens from entering and protecting the rest of the plant. However, that's not all—plant cells also launch a counter-attack by releasing Hydrogen Peroxide and Nitric Oxide. These chemicals signal a series of biochemical reactions that ultimately lead to the death of the host cells in the affected area. Essentially, it's like the plant's defense army, swiftly responding to threats to keep itself safe and healthy[8].

This plant response system indicates their preparedness for the future through foresight and insight into what is happening inside their internal system. The same characteristic, when imbibed in the organizational culture of the business, can enable them to be prepared for future uncertainties while at the same time being mindful of the threats around them. Conventionally, strategic planning has been adopted in organizations to deal with the uncertainties around them. It starts with asking questions like "where are we at present?" followed by "what do we want to do next?".

However, a transition from traditional strategic planning to strategic foresight involves being able to eliminate the restrictions and boundaries of "where are we at present", instead enriching the context in which the development, planning, and execution of the strategy are taking place. Strategic foresight involves various tools that can be used to identify and study the internal and external drivers of change while scanning through the horizon to identify new emerging trends and those that are anonymous. By studying unknown trends, organizations can gain more insight into their uncertainties.

Scenario planning is another way organizations can identify insights by studying the unknown trends and then translating the information to guide the alternatives for a likely future by interpreting those signals that might impact their businesses.

Navigating Uncertainty, Learning From Venus Flytrap

Charles Darwin called the Venus Flytrap (Dionaea muscipula) "one of the most wonderful plants in the world." Do you know why?

Simply because of its ability to rapidly close its leaf within 100 ms, which is one of the fastest movements in the plant kingdom[9].

Don't you feel businesses must develop a similar internal mechanism that enables them to navigate uncertain situations with agility and respond quickly?

The simple mechanism by which the Venus Flytrap plant seizes its prey inside its leaves is by altering the shape of its leaves to store potential mechanical energy that can be released when it needs to trigger trap closure[10]. This plant can open its trap by simply stretching its leaves back on themselves. While stretching, it can store its potential energy as elastic energy. As soon as the plant senses any element on its surface that could be a threat, it immediately triggers the leaf to shut, and hydraulic movement in the leaves releases the stored energy, causing the trap to snap close over its prey[10]. Returning to the original shape is where the prey gets trapped. This entire process happens in about 10 ms, isn't it too rapid? This swiftness is needed to survive whenever there is a disturbance or imbalance in the ecosystem.

The COVID-19 pandemic was when all the people and organizations expected such a swift response to survive the harsh times and thrive in them. Learning from the Venus flytrap plants, the startups should also keep their internal system robust but flexible to alter their organizational functioning during uncertain times. Not only this, they should also be expeditious while responding to the threats around them. Pivoting during uncertain times is the most crucial to survive amidst the unfavorable.

Amidst the global pandemic, numerous companies swiftly adapted and pivoted their strategies to navigate the uncertainties, ensuring their survival in the face of unprecedented challenges.

One such company was Snapbar, which was an events service company pre-pandemic. Since the world shut down overnight with no events during COVID-19, this company pivoted its business within a week to a gift box company[11]. They launched an entirely new stream of business that integrates gift boxes containing products sourced from local businesses. They contacted the local vendors and businesses and assembled a box called "Keep Your City Smiling." These were city-specific boxes launched in Seattle, Los Angeles, and San Francisco, personalized for undergraduates and healthcare workers based on their specific requirements. This agile pivot enabled them to survive the ravages of time.

Similarly, many other companies also diversified their revenue streams; some raised funding, added new product lines, and some took this opportunity to launch their online businesses, etc[12]. All those businesses that survived amidst the pandemic were those whose response was quick and efficacious. This agile pivot allowed them to weather the storm and thrive in adversity. Likewise, numerous other companies diversified their revenue streams, securing funding, introducing new product lines, and seizing the opportunity to establish their presence online. The common thread among these resilient businesses was their swift and effective response to the challenges posed by the pandemic.

WIRELESS STIMULATION: DRIVING THE ORGANIZATION

Unlike animals and human beings, plants are immobile living creatures. Are they immobile just because they cannot move much from where they are rooted? Not really. Even though they cannot show complex movements, they have adapted ways to demonstrate mobility in their simple lifestyle to reproduce, compete with other plants for resources, adapt to their environment, and avoid or defend themselves from herbivores[13].

The various ways by which plants show movement is called tropism, which could be either due to gravity (gravitropism), physical touch (thigmotropism), or in response to light (phototropism), or alteration in water pressure (hydrotropism) and many others. Although they cannot relocate, these simple movements allow the plants to defy the fact that they are completely immobile. Despite their stationary nature, plants demonstrate remarkable adaptability through these movements. Their ability to respond to external stimuli, such as gravity, sunlight, touch, or water, allows them to overcome immobility. Surprisingly, sunlight can influence a plant's movement toward its source, even without direct contact.

But how does this occur?

The sunlight triggers a wireless stimulation within the plant, not only in its stem but also in its branches and attached leaves and leaflets. The sunlight modifies the growth of these stems and branches, making the plant bend toward the light. Auxins are hormones within the plant responsible for its stimulatory response towards light. Auxins surge in the plant parts that receive less light; this results in the elongation of cells in those areas through a weakening of the rigid cell wall and an increase in the cell's water intake[13]. Thus, this leads to the bending of the plant stem towards the sun, and it shifts as and when the direction of the Sun changes throughout the day.

Imagine if a Sun can wirelessly stimulate and manage a plant's movement; what impact can a leader have on the growth and movement of the organization? A leader embodies energy, brightness, and courage, guiding and propelling the company forward. Just like a Sun can direct a plant's movement, a leader can make things happen by exerting intrinsic and extrinsic influences on all the stakeholders in an organization. In today's dynamic business landscape, stability is a luxury few organizations enjoy. Market trends, customer demands, and technological advancements are in constant flux. Therefore, organizations require adept leaders who can harness this energy, unlock potential, and steer them toward success. A leader in an organization enables the people to overcome challenges by providing them with a shared vision of where the organization is heading and its purpose (the mission)[14]. Through strategic goal-setting, they can focus on critical areas crucial for success, driving performance and productivity.

Moreover, like a wireless stimulator, a leader offers strategic guidance, empowering employees to leverage their expertise for the organization's growth and development.

With all these lessons from the plant world, startups can imbibe a culture of flexibility, leadership, and strategic foresight to manage uncertain, complex, and ambiguous situations effectively and efficiently. Preparedness is an often-mentioned but frequently ignored necessity to break free from frozen habits to make organizations thrive.

Just as "Touch-me-not" shields from surprise,

Startups adapt, foreseeing highs and lows arise.

Like Venus flytrap, they seize opportunities near

Insight and foresight, their growth pioneers.

– Amya Madan

PART 3

SEED TO TREE = IDEAS TO IMPACT

11.

SYNERGY

CONVERGING PARALLELS BETWEEN PLANT ANATOMY AND BUSINESS UNITS

"Alone we can do so little; together we can do so much."

– Helen Keller

Which part of the plant prepares its food- the stem or the leaves? Is chloroplast known as the "powerhouse of plants"? But why?

Which plant part helps transport water and minerals from the soil to the other parts- the xylem or phloem?

Well! All these questions have a unique answer because each cell and tissue inside the plant performs a different function and plays a unique role, but in harmony to enable the plant's survival. Not all plant parts are involved in making food, and not all are involved in transporting water. Anatomically, a plant is a complex system of simple and complex tissues working together to perform several functions and make plants a living species.

Have you ever drawn a plant or a tree on paper? Isn't it effortless? Just a trunk with some branches and leaves bearing fruits and flowers. Physiologically, a plant may be easy to draw, but anatomically, plants are not so simple; they comprise a complex system of tissues that controls and manages all the functions inside the plant.

Even though plants can't move around like animals, they're also made up of cells, tissues, and organs. Plants have two main organs: the shoot and the root. The shoot is the part of the plant above the ground, while the roots are buried underground. These organs play a significant role in the growth and development of plants. Inside the plant are different tissues that help move water and food around. Xylem tissues carry water and minerals from the roots to the rest of the plant, while phloem tissues transport food. Inside the leaves is the powerhouse of the plants known as "chloroplast". They are called so because they are the site of photosynthesis in plants, which provides food and energy to the plant by using sunlight and carbon dioxide and giving out energy to all life forms on Earth.

How beautifully and in a synchronized way all the plant tissues function and play their specific roles to aid a plant in its growth and development.

Learning Lessons From Plant Tissues

Can startups learn anything from these plant tissues?

What is analogous to tissues in an organization that forms an integral part of its growth story?

What are the different roles each performs, and how can their synchronicity help startups succeed?

Plants around us hold the answers to these questions. We can unlock these secrets by dissecting a plant and studying its anatomy. Similarly, while startups have a clear vision and mission to make a difference, there's often more happening behind the scenes than meets the eye.

Within an organization, different departments handle various tasks, each contributing to the overall business objectives. Like different parts of a plant, these departments work together in harmony. Like plants, startups have different departments, such as human resources, operations, marketing, sales, finance, innovation, and research and development. A tissue that protects the plant cannot transport water from one part to another in a plant or vice versa. This signifies that the function of each tissue is unique yet integral for the proper functioning of a plant. Just as certain tissues in a plant have specific functions, like protecting the plant or transporting water, each department in a startup has its unique role. For instance, the functions performed by the marketing team in an organization cannot be performed by the finance team, but that doesn't alter the fact that both are equally required by the business to function at their best potential.

A plant without phloem tissues will die because even if the leaves prepare the food, there will be no channel to transport that food from the leaves to other plant parts. It's like a delivery truck without roads; there's no way to transport the prepared food from leaves to other parts of the plant. If a plant lacks chloroplasts, it can't make food in the first place, so there's no need for phloem tissues. This illustrates the importance of every business unit working in unison. Just as every part of a plant is vital for its survival, each department in a business plays a crucial role in its growth and success. Think of it like a team sport where every player has a specific role. Depending on the company's needs and size, some areas might have more team members than others. For example, big companies like Nike and Apple have extensive Research and Development (R&D) teams to stay ahead in their industries.

On the other hand, retail companies might not focus as much on R&D but will put much effort into operations, like managing their supply chain[1]. When each business function performs well, the company runs smoothly and efficiently.

A tree trunk is the central control system that connects its upper and underground parts. It also stands firm, protecting all plant tissues. Analogous to the tree trunk is the management team in a startup that plays a vital role in keeping the business running smoothly. They act as the central control unit, providing protection and guidance to all other functions. Just as a trunk gives a tree its structure, the management team ensures that everyone in the company knows what they need to do and how to communicate effectively. They supervise the performance of all employees, track achievements, set goals, and make plans to help the company grow. In short, they ensure all resources are used efficiently to help the startup succeed.

Another integral team in running a business is its 'Marketing' department.

The marketing function of startups is analogous to the 'xylem' in plants. The xylem tissues in a plant are responsible for transporting water and minerals from the roots to all plant parts. Correspondingly, the marketing team's role is not only to strategize ways of selling the product, but their primary responsibility is to identify the problems and needs of the people and address them to the management so that they can create an impact through their solution profitably. Just the way the xylem tissues go into the depth of the roots to absorb water and take it uphill to the tip of the leaves. Similarly, the role of the marketing team is to dive deep into the gravity of the problem, understand the pain points that might not be visible on the surface of the people's lifestyle, and then pass them over to the 'Innovation' team so that they devise a solution which can benefit the whole ecosystem. The water absorbed by the roots and transported by the xylem not only fulfills the water and nutrient needs of the plant but also completes the water cycle by getting evaporated from the stomatal openings of the leaves. This is precisely how the marketing team functions, which brings the pain points of the customers into the system of the startup and then also carries the solution back into the ecosystem for the overall benefit of the customers by conceptualizing and strategizing ways to market the product by either branding the startup or advertising it in the right way so that more and more people buy it.

Marketing also involves promoting the final products/services through various channels, including digital marketing. This function is also responsible for governing the decisions on how these products will be transported, where they will be promoted, and the price point. As we become a technology-driven world, the role of marketing has expanded in managing the online presence through the social media channels which drive major e-commerce companies, mobile banking as well as service-technology companies. The marketing teams within an organization must also be careful of their offline vs. online strategies for the company's product/service. Without offline resources, online might seem to be the best course of action to transition from brick-and-mortar stores to e-commerce platforms. Government partnerships also play a crucial role in this shift. For instance, ONDC (Open Network for Digital Commerce) would allow small business owners and retailers to avail the benefits of the digital world and sell their products/services to benefit the customers without the need to bother about the high cost of commissions involved with the big players like Amazon, Zomato etc[2].

The xylem tissues in plants can only transport water and minerals from the roots to the leaves, it is the stomatal pores that enable the transportation of water from the leaves into the atmosphere. That means the marketing team can only provide a channel to reach the market, but there is a different function that sells the product/service and closes the deal with the customers. The 'Sales' team, which is equivalent to the stomatal pores in a plant, plays that function in a business. The sales team's role is to work on the leads created by the marketing team and convert them into potential clients for the company. This team in a startup is directly linked to creating revenues. Let's consider that this revenue is like carbon dioxide in the atmosphere. To bring in revenue, the sales team has to give out (sell) the product to the customers in the ecosystem and, in turn, bring profits within the organization. It works in the exact same way as the stomatal pores function. They give out the oxygen (a product/service for the utility of the customers) and take in the carbon dioxide (the revenue) to perform photosynthesis (which is the overall existence of the company). In the absence of carbon dioxide, a plant cannot prepare food. Without money, a startup cannot perform all the functions required for sustenance. The sales team has the competency to persuade the customers to buy their products. Without a sales team, the company cannot increase its reach to a broader set of customers.

The phloem tissues in a plant are responsible for transporting the food prepared by the leaves to other plant parts and providing them with the required nutrients and energy in the form of food for further growth, elongation, and maturation. This is called Translocation according to the anatomical terminology of plants.

Who performs this function for a startup?

The logistics and operations team is responsible for transporting the end products to the customers and the specific business units. Food cannot be transported within a cell without a phloem; without the operations team, the products cannot reach customers. Operations is the functional unit in a business where the input is converted into the output and is finally transported through a well-defined supply chain to the specific parts. Unlike the xylem, which can only move in one direction, i.e. unidirectional, the phloem tissues are bidirectional and can move up and down from source to sink. This is precisely how the logistics and operations team in a startup functions. Their role is not only to transport or deliver the products from the warehouse to the customer but also to bring the defective pieces or rejected products back to the company from the customer's source. That is why their function is not uni-directional but rather multidirectional.

Some other tissues between the xylem and phloem help in the growth and development of these tissues.

How does a business manage its marketing and operations team?

Who is responsible for forming and developing these functional units in a business?

Again, let's draw a parallel between the plant tissues responsible for forming the xylem and phloem tissues and the business units in the organization that support the marketing and sales teams.

The company's Human Resources (HR) department is analogous to Cambium. The tissue supports the formation of the xylem and phloem whenever there is a dearth or rupturing of these tissues due to internal or external pressure. The HR team of a company performs a similar role in the organization's functioning. Their job is to find and hire the right people for different jobs in the company, like marketing, operations, finance, and sales. Once hired, they also track how well these employees do their jobs. They decide things like bonuses and promotions based on their performance, similar to how xylem and phloem tissues mature and develop in plants. Essentially, the HR department helps manage all employees and ensures the company gets the right people on board.

Although HRs talk about the KPIs – Key Performance Indicators, while evaluating the performance of the employees for appraisals, there is a need to shift this focus. Instead of the Key Performance Indicators, HRs should focus on fulfilling the novel acronym for these KPIs– ***Keep People Innovative, Keep People Interested, Keep People Informed.*** Achieving these KPIs, along with the conventional ones, will inspire employees to contribute more toward the company's expansion.

As the company's management acts as a protective outer layer of the tree, there is another layer in the plant, which is the innermost layer but performs an essential function of selectively taking in the nutrients they need while filtering out the harmful materials found in soil. This innermost layer of the plant is visible only after passing through several outer layers. The companies also have a similar innermost team – the 'Finance' department of the business. These are the people who together form the functional unit of the business, who have the slightest interaction with the outer ecosystem but perform the core function of managing the accounts, the expenditure, revenue, and profits of the company, just the way the internal layer of the plant does – selectively deciding selection and rejection of the nutrients that it wants inside the cell. Accuracy is the core function of the finance team. Entry of a single harmful material into the cell due to the negligence of this layer can have enormous repercussions for the plants. Negligence or error of the finance team can similarly cause negative fallouts for the company. The finance department is responsible for everything related to money – managing the organization's cash and bank accounts, maintaining accurate transaction records, and preparing final accounts[3]. Precise financial record-keeping is essential for a company to avoid legal problems. Even though the finance team's work might not be visible to customers, it is vital for the organization's smooth operation. Their job ensures that the company doesn't run out of money or face issues with unregulated financial transactions.

INNOVATION FUELS AN ORGANIZATION'S SUCCESS

The food for the plant drives all its functions. The plant cannot function properly, no matter how tall or sturdy, without food.

The tree's stability can also waiver if it doesn't make food for many days. Just like food fuels a plant's growth and functions, innovation fuels the success of startups. Without innovation, companies can't thrive or adapt to market changes. The innovation department is like the kitchen of a business – the food-making unit, creating new ideas and products by collaborating with research, development, and marketing teams. This constant stream of new ideas keeps the company competitive and relevant in the ever-changing market.

Like chloroplasts, innovation is the powerhouse of any startup as it helps them to achieve their competitive advantage. Startups equipped with an innovation unit or a culture of innovation tend to outlast their competitors, as innovation provides the essential fuel for long-term survival and success. Innovation is not specific to a business function; it permeates the organization and can influence every aspect of its operations. When coupled with innovation, the marketing team can devise creative and unconventional strategies to promote and brand their products effectively, giving the startup a competitive edge in the market. Integrating innovation with the HR department can empower them to explore fresh and novel methods for recruiting and selecting candidates. It serves as the lifeblood of all organizational functions within a startup. Without innovation, these functional units would stagnate, leading the company toward gradual decline and eventual demise.

A simple example to illustrate the importance of innovation is a conventional shoe-making company creating footwear with sizes 5 through 9. However, with some innovation, some startups devised novel ways of branding their shoes communicating that their footwear is available in sizes such as 6.5 or 9.5. This innovative approach caters to customers who don't fall within the standard size range, offering them a better fit and addressing their needs.

Moreover, innovation has extended beyond product development to HR practices. For instance, companies are leveraging artificial intelligence software to streamline the hiring process. This software scans through resumes, filtering candidates based on specific keywords relevant to the job role, enhancing efficiency and accuracy in recruitment.

STRONG ROOTS MEAN NO FEAR OF WINDS.

In plants, the root cap is a layer of cells that forms the outermost part of the root tip, facilitating smooth movement into the soil depths. For startups, their research and development teams serve as their root cap, delving deep into the reality of people and their preferences and acting as a conduit between the marketing team and customers. The xylem cannot transport the water from the roots to the leaves unless the roots absorb water from the soil. Just as the roots absorb water for the xylem to transport, R&D provides essential data for the marketing team to identify customer needs. This collaborative effort between R&D and marketing is crucial in mapping the customer journey and developing practical solutions.

Additionally, the R&D team fosters collaboration among innovators, scientists, industry experts, leaders, and customers, driving the company's growth and development.

As we explored the anatomy of plants, we discovered the diverse and vital roles played by each tissue and structure.

Similarly, various functional units operate independently yet collaboratively within a business to drive company growth. Just as every part of a plant has its unique function, each business unit contributes to the overall success, highlighting the importance of teamwork. No function can perform all the roles alone.

TEAMWORK- CRITICAL TO A STARTUP'S SUCCESS

A startup is a repertoire of ideas, creativity, and an amalgamation of people working under the same roof, under diverse working conditions, and robust operations to impact the market by creating an innovative product.

Regardless of the efficiency of operations, the clarity of roles, or the availability of funding and expertise, a startup's success hinges on teamwork. Even the most well-designed systems can collapse without collaboration and cooperation among team members.

Within a startup, novel ideas proliferate, and some people learn and hone new skills.

These are a close bunch of enthusiastic individuals with mutual trust and harmony who work together to achieve a collective goal. But snap! All of this can rupture within seconds if there is no teamwork among the people. This can happen only when one indispensable precondition is met: teamwork or, precisely, good teamwork[4]. Good teamwork enables a startup not only to survive but also to thrive under extreme conditions. In the fast-paced world of startups, time is often scarce, and tasks are tackled simultaneously, sometimes overlapping. Maintaining teamwork among all employees is crucial in this scenario to prevent chaos. By fostering a culture of collaboration and synchronization, startups can harness the diverse expertise of their team members to work toward a common goal, ensuring efficient workflow and collective success. With good teamwork, each can learn something from the other and perform to their highest potential together.

Oh, do you know? Chloroplasts in the plants prepare their food,

But without the stomatal pores, I can't let the water extrude.

In the absence of one part, the other cannot survive,

*That's why all functional areas are crucial for your
business to thrive.*

– Amya Madan

12.

VENTURING BOLDLY
EMBRACING RISKS, REAPING REWARDS

The biggest risk is not taking any risk.

– Mark Zuckerburg

A farmer in the field is frequently exposed to weather, prices, and disease uncertainties. In developing countries, the chances of survival are sometimes just above the threshold; in others, they are just at the edge of falling below the threshold[1]. A farmer does not know whether the rainfall over this season will be good or bad, neither is he assured of the prices he will receive for his produce. He is uncertain whether he can produce a good crop or if his crops will be infected by disease even before reaping. However, do these uncertainties and risks stop farmers from growing crops yearly and sowing fresh seeds? No. Farmers do not have control over all these environmental conditions and risks, but they have developed ways of coping with and managing them over the years. This risk management allows them to produce healthy crops.

Farming is risky, and so is en-tree-preneurship. Commercialization of farming has made it riskier for the farmers. Every day, the farmers have to make several decisions that cannot be predicted with 100% accuracy but are critical for everyday farming operations. Production of crops can easily be affected by risks, which include sudden changes in weather, attacks from pests, and diseases. Equipment breakdown can also pose a challenge as much as market price fluctuations can. Additionally, changes in the interest rate of borrowed money and governmental policies can also majorly impact farmers' produce. Nevertheless, no matter what, for their survival and growth, the farmers have to deal with these risks, manage them efficiently, and make decisions. Similarly, an entrepreneur has to face many challenges while nurturing his idea to create an impact. The everyday risks of logistics and operations, the changing market trends, environmental conditions, technological advancements, the economic situation, managing finances, raising investments, etc. pose many challenges and involve significant risk. However, the success of a startup depends upon navigating these challenges through efficient risk management and sound decision-making abilities.

Farmers, like anyone else in business, have varying attitudes toward risk. Some are cautious, avoiding risky ventures, while others are more adventurous and willing to take chances for potential gains. However, there is also a middle ground—farmers who balance caution and risk-taking. They are called risk-neutral, and they carefully assess situations and weigh the benefits against the dangers before making decisions. They draw from experience, past outcomes, and available information to manage risks effectively. While higher risks can lead to higher profits, they also demand careful handling. Effective risk management involves anticipating potential problems and developing strategies to minimize their impact; it is not about reacting hastily but making informed decisions to navigate challenges successfully.

For farmers, decision-making starts from the point when they have to decide which crop to grow at the start of a season.

They have to make every single decision, from what to plant, how much to plant, and when. These decisions might appear trivial but can have catastrophic effects if gone wrong. This is because every decision leads to a consequence unknown to the farmer at the time of the decision.

The sources of these risks can vary from production to technical, marketing to financial, and institutional to human errors.

1. The **production risk** begins when the farmer fertilizes and sows the seed. At that time, they are unaware of how much it will rain in that season and whether there will be droughts, floods, or hail storms. But still, they are determined to sow the seeds and grow the crop. They spend enormous amounts of money and resources plowing the soil, tilling it, and preparing it for sowing the seeds.

2. The **technical risk** involves the sudden breakdown of their equipment. Imagine a farmer plowing the ground to sow the seeds, and suddenly, the tractor stops functioning. This would result in the inability to harvest in time, thus affecting the yield.

3. Even if the farmer produces a good crop, the **marketing risk** is still beyond their control as the demand and supply of the crop influence it. All of this is variable because it depends on cyclical changes, government policies, inflation, and seasonal demands.

4. The **financial risk** comes into the picture when farmers have to borrow or take loans, which they usually have to. The risk in this situation is caused by precariousness about future interest rates, the lender's willingness to provide funds when needed, and the farmer's ability to generate sufficient income to repay the loan and support his family. This situation worsens for small or medium farmers,

coerced to borrow money at high interest rates, leading to their inability to repay debt.

5. The **institutional risks** are borne by the fluctuation of government and subsidiaries and the withdrawal of services offered by banks and cooperatives. These risks can affect the farmer beyond his control and sometimes lead them to sell off their land to repay the old debts.

6. The **human or personal risk** further exacerbates the risks in farming caused by the illness, injury, or death of the farmer or his family members. Migration also poses problems, which makes labor management difficult.

Managing risks effectively is crucial for a fruitful harvest, regardless of their origin. However, the nature of risks faced by farmers can differ significantly, making it challenging to adopt a one-size-fits-all strategy. For instance, farmers relying on rainfall may face the looming threat of drought, while those cultivating exotic fruits may be more concerned about market prices. Consequently, their decisions to mitigate risks vary based on the specific challenges they encounter and their severity. Time management is also a critical factor in managing risks. The timing of a farmer's decisions is crucial in managing risks effectively. Whether it's the immediate impacts or the long-term consequences, both play a significant role. Thus, they must make decisions that address short-term needs while also considering broader, long-term strategies to ensure their operations remain sustainable and resilient in the face of uncertainties.

Risk management and decision-making is an iterative cycle that holds true for entrepreneurs and their startups as well. While the future can look bright, it can be rife with risks. Entrepreneurs and CEOs must thrive in their businesses despite these risks and uncertainties. For entrepreneurs, risk management matters because a wrong decision can have menacing outcomes for them.

Starting from the technical, production, human, institutional, and financial risks, they have to manage it all by making decisions discreetly. In order to grow, startups should refrain from formulating a strategy to avoid risk; instead, they should learn early identification and management of risk.

Consider a farmer planting mango seeds in the summer, anticipating a bountiful harvest. However, when the mangoes ripen, it's winter and demand for mangoes plummets. This scenario mirrors the plight of startups. Often, founders fall in love with their ideas without considering the actual needs of their customers. Consequently, when they introduce their product to the market, they discover – it doesn't resonate with consumers. This misalignment leads to wasted resources, money, and time. To mitigate these risks, startups are increasingly adopting Lean principles for more effective risk management.

LEAN PRINCIPLES FOR BETTER RISK MANAGEMENT

Lean fundamentally has seven main principles[2].

These are:

1. optimize the whole

2. eliminate waste

3. build quality in

4. learn constantly

5. deliver fast

6. engage everyone

7. keep getting better

Henry Ford followed the style of mass production. In contrast, these principles emerged from the lean manufacturing concept used by the Japanese Toyota that adopted a new system, enabling them to produce automobiles with almost half the labor hours and much faster inventory.

This system enabled Toyota to do Just-in-Time (JIT) final assembly and shipment to dealers eliminating most of the excess inventories. Traditionally, the startups used a waterfall model to test their startup by dividing the project into different stages, allowing the project owners to decide between abandoning the project or moving on to the next stage. However, with current time and budget constraints, the startups have begun implementing Lean principles. This enables them to minimize waste in terms of time and money by simply creating more value for customers with fewer resources[3].

The Lean Product Cycle is different from the conventional cycle of product development. Instead of directly launching the product in the market, they first build the **Minimum Viable Product**, a testing version of the new product that allows a team to collect the maximum amount of validated learning about customers with the least effort. After several rounds of testing the MVP, they iterate their hypothesis and bring about changes in their original MVP until they finally launch their product. Lean development involves constantly improving the product to bring maximum customer value by eliminating waste and continuously learning from customer feedback. In this way, the risk of dissipating large sums of money for building and launching a product in the market that no one wants is curtailed.

Instead, when the products are built according to customers' needs and pain points, startups can sell their products and maintain a successful business.

A successful startup that used these lean principles for its benefit was DropBox. In 2007, when Dropbox began its entrepreneurial journey, its co-founders, Drew Houston and Arash Ferdowsi, just constructed a simple landing page that explained their product to the customers[4]. Though they received 5,000 signups initially, more was needed for them to decide to build a product. A significant leap came in the number of signups from 5,000 to 75,000 when they launched a 3-minute video that acted as a demo for their product "DropBox." Instead of building a product by utilizing their money, energy, and resources, which the people might not like, this video enabled them to measure people's interest in their product. Due to the growing interest in their product, the founders of Dropbox decided to continue the development process. Dropbox reached 1 million users in 7 months, and in 15 months, in January 2010, it reached 4 million registered users[4]. Over time, they also realized that referrals worked best for them. So, they bought some pivots in their online marketing strategies to cut customer acquisition costs and give importance to referrals.

A similar Lean principle strategy was adopted by Zappos, a company that started in 1999, much before online shopping became a buzzword. They wanted to know whether or not people were interested in buying shoes online[5]. Building a new e-commerce website, marinating an inventory of shoes, and managing the logistics and distribution would have cost many resources and money to its co-founders. Instead of taking this risk, they applied the lean model of launching an MVP. In their case, the MVP was their website. They collaborated with local shoe stores, took pictures of their products, and uploaded these pictures as an online display for their customers. Thus, by running an online campaign to buy shoes online through their website, they could understand people's interest and later launched a full-fledged website that was then sold to Amazon for a billion dollars[6].

These case studies exemplify the effectiveness of implementing Lean principles in startups to mitigate risks efficiently. By embracing Lean methodologies, startups can minimize wastage of time, money, and resources while maximizing customer value. By soliciting and incorporating customer feedback at every crucial stage of product development, startups can ensure that their final product aligns perfectly with customer needs. This proactive approach minimizes risks and enhances the likelihood of successful product launches, ultimately driving increased sales and customer satisfaction.

The Build-Measure-Learn strategy is well-applicable to almost all entrepreneurial ventures. This is because the fundamental activity of a startup is to turn ideas into innovative products, measure how customers acknowledge them, and then learn whether to pivot or persevere. All successful startup processes should be geared to accelerate that feedback loop[7].

Entrepreneurship is not restricted to a particular garage or office; it is ubiquitous. Any human institution designed to create new products and services under extreme uncertainty can be called a startup[7]. This means entrepreneurs are everywhere, and the 'Lean Startup approach' can be used in any size. Economic, political, and environmental changes can often pose challenges for startups spreading their roots in the market. These challenging, life-changing situations demand them to weigh the risks and options before deciding and choosing accordingly.

EVEN PEA PLANTS ARE RISK-TAKERS.

Startups can learn adaptive response mechanisms from plants that demonstrate risk management and decision-making even without a nervous system. Even without a nervous system like other living organisms, plants still make good decisions for survival[8]. This was proved through an experiment when a Pea plant, *Pisum sativum*, was tested to measure its response to risks. Initially, in the first set of conditions, the pea plant was grown such that its roots were split into two different pots.

One of the pots had more nutrients than the other; thus, the pea plant also grew more roots in the pot with more nutrients. Good decision. Indeed! But the way these plants make eerily good decisions under risky circumstances was demonstrated in the next phase when the pea plant was now grown in two pots under varying conditions. Under one instance, the roots of the pea plant were split into two pots, one having steadily high nutrients while the other one having a varying supply of nutrients, wavering from high to low yet averaging to the same constant high level of the first pot. The results showed that these pea plants were risk-averse and thus grew more roots in the pot with a steady supply of nutrients.

In another instance, the roots of the pea plants were split into two different pots. But this time, one of the pots had steadily low nutrients while the supply of nutrients in the other pot varied, ranging from low to high, but the average being as low as the first pot. This resulted in the plants taking a more challenging decision of growing more roots in the pot with a variable supply of nutrients compared to the one with a constant low supply. Why? Because they became risk-takers in this situation.

Both these decisions are well-thought-out by the plants and suitable for survival. The plant was getting a constant high supply of nutrients in the first case, but in the second, taking the risk of growing roots in the variable pot was a gamble on the streak to try good luck instead of putting effort into managing with the low nutrients. This is similar to how humans think and organizations with risk-taking abilities function. If someone offers an organization a guaranteed $700, or a coin flip that yields $1,200 for heads and nothing for tails, most people would consider going with the first option as it would yield a constant higher average payout. But what if the company is stranded without money and needs $1000 to start operations? Flipping the coin for a chance at $1,200 could be more logical. This is what makes it a good decision. These decisions are as crucial for an organization as they are for growing plants. If plants without a nervous system can take such a premeditated decision, organizations and humans with a well-developed nervous system can develop risk-taking abilities to excel.

This example is an excellent evidence of how organizations should develop sensitivity to variability in resources[9]. Growing startups and companies should switch between risk proneness and risk aversion depending on the state and circumstances. This comparison can be relevant to emerging startups facing challenges along their journey. Sometimes, startups secure enough funds, but as they grow, they must decide whether to expand into new market segments. This decision involves risks like spending money, managing operations, and choosing which market to enter. They may have to choose between a market with consistently low demand or one where demand fluctuates. Making wise decisions entails taking risks expanding into markets with more customers and better growth prospects, despite the uncertainties.

A straightforward analogy exists between the risks faced by the farmers while sowing the seeds for a new crop and a new idea launched by an entrepreneur. Both have to go through periods of uncertainties and thoughtful decision-making before they reap the results of what they have sown. Though the risks they would face during their journey cannot be predicted, they can be efficiently managed with a good risk management strategy and diligent decision-making. There is no ONE mantra for risk management. However, over the years, by studying the market trends and statistical data, new strategies for risk management can be devised so that organizations become risk-takers, not risk-aversive. A prepared mindset can help entrepreneurs mitigate the catastrophic effects of uncertainties if proper risk management strategies are adopted, which can benefit the owners and stakeholders.

There are days when I need to decide

Whether to bloom, or in the bud I should hide.

I decide to take risks, no matter how cumbersome,

That's how you'll see me grow & blossom.

– Amya Madan

13.

SEASONAL ADAPTATIONS
NAVIGATING MARKET SHIFTS

Winter is an etching, spring a watercolor,

Summer an oil paint, and autumn, a mosaic of all.

– Stanley Horowitz

Every changing season brings opportunities for the plants to change. Adapting to these seasonal changes enables the plants to bloom even more, grow taller, and produce the season's best fruits. Change is the only constant for plants, and so is for businesses and startups that face a dynamic environment where adaptation is vital to survival and growth. Embracing change allows them to flourish, reach new heights, and yield the best results, much like the fruits of a well-adapted plant. In both nature and business, change is constant, and those who embrace it are the ones who thrive.

All the plants around, whether in the open field or a garden, know how to detect seasonal changes and adapt to them very well. With every month that passes, the season changes a bit, which causes plants to make several noticeable and latent alterations to survive. As days become shorter and nights become longer, plants also begin showing profound changes in how they grow and behave.

It may seem simplistic to think trees have a built-in mechanism to adapt to external factors like temperature, daylight hours, soil quality, and rainfall, however, this ability allows them to survive and thrive for many years, adapting to changing conditions to ensure their continued growth and resilience.

As the Earth travels around the Sun, the length of day and night fluctuates, bringing about seasonal changes. Plants can very well detect these changes, and thus, they know when to bloom depending on the duration of the night. Plants get triggered by these seasonal changes because of the presence of pigments that allow them to measure light over 24 hours. Various hormones are secreted inside the plant based on this light exposure and duration of the night, which either leads to the formation of a bulb, makes it bloom, or sheds its leaves, all of which are activated by these hormones. Similarly, plants have a detection mechanism that allows them to respond to the changing temperatures around them. For example, as spring nears, peach trees and azaleas measure how cold the atmosphere is and for how long. After a certain number of cold hours, these plants have an internal mechanism that causes them to grow or bloom[1].

In addition to the inherent changes occurring naturally in trees, farmers must make strategic decisions to adjust to seasonal shifts by choosing plants or seed varieties suitable for specific seasons. They need to tend to crops currently in season and anticipate and prepare for upcoming seasonal changes. Therefore, knowing what to plant both in the present and the future, based on seasonal transitions, is essential to ensure continuous growth and productivity throughout the year.

As summer transitions into winter, passing through the fall season, farmers often opt to grow shrubs or trees that enter a dormant stage but hold the promise of blooming again during spring. Planting such seeds typically occurs during autumn since the soil becomes challenging to work with during winter, either due to the cold or excessive water saturation, making nutrient absorption difficult.

Consequently, instead of planting during the harsh winter months, farmers focus on protecting their crops. Then, as spring arrives, the dormant bulbs planted back in early winter start to bloom, bursting forth in vibrant colors as summer approaches and soil conditions become optimal for growth.

Like a farmer carefully selecting the right crops for each season, entrepreneurs must also choose the appropriate sector for launching their startup. This decision hinges on various factors, including current market trends and the evolving lifestyle preferences of consumers. Here, I draw a sharp analogy between how plants adapt to shifting seasonal conditions and how startups must pivot and flourish amidst changing market dynamics and evolving consumer preferences.

While it may seem daunting to keep up with the ever-changing market landscape and consumer demands, that's what we must learn from plants' resilience and adaptability, right?

Have you ever seen lilac bushes being crushed by snow drifts during winter?

If yes, you must have also seen them blooming again on a warm day a few weeks later. That is precisely how plants tolerate extreme changing conditions, but they come back more beautifully by adapting to these changes and responding most effectively. Animals have a way to escape the chilly winter storms by hibernating, and human beings have warm clothes to wear to endure the cold during winter. However, plants can neither hibernate nor escape. They have to stand tall and face it.

Over the centuries, trees have devised tricks to survive frigid temperatures. During autumn, woody plants in many parts of the world start preparing for winter. When their leaves change color and fall, their twigs, branches, and trunks start losing water. As a result, the concentration of sugars, salts, and organic compounds in their cells increases, eventually lowering the freezing point of the cells and tissues. This allows them to survive temperatures far below the average freezing point of water[2]. During winter, the trees maintain a temperature at or above freezing point around their roots. The soil, fallen leaves, and persistent snow layers insulate the ground above the roots and prevent it from losing heat. Not just that, plants also have advanced wake-up call systems. They do not start re-growing fresh leaves instantaneously; instead, they have a specific mechanism to decide when to start blooming again and end their dormancy. Other plants start growing as soon as they receive a certain number of warm days during the early spring, while others have a photoperiod response, which allows them to prepare for the growth of fresh leaves based on the length of time and duration for which they are exposed to light. As and when days get longer and warmer in the spring, they begin reacting to seasonal changes by breaking their dormancy and shooting fresh leaves.

In the ever-changing world of industries, entrepreneurs must navigate the dynamic trends while juggling daily operations. However, staying ahead of the curve and preempting market shifts is crucial to outpace competitors. While farmers anticipate the upcoming season, they cannot predict its exact intensity or challenges for their crops.

Nevertheless, they continue preparing the soil and sowing seeds, choosing varieties that thrive in specific conditions.

Similarly, entrepreneurs must understand diverse market patterns and techniques to select strategies that align with anticipated trends, ensuring they remain adaptable and resilient in the face of uncertainty.

Market trend analysis works on similar lines. Analyzing market trends is not as scary as it sounds to be. It simply means studying and comparing the industrial data and consumer behavior over time and then recognizing the trends that have remained consistent and paying no heed to those that have either vanished or have been disrupted due to transformation in people's lifestyles[3]. Mapping all these market trends and connecting the dots can help an entrepreneur design a business strategy that aligns with the current market needs of the target segment. If studied carefully, it can be noticed that the market trends enormously depend upon consumers and are highly influenced by consumer habits, behaviors, and lifestyles. Thus, in today's digital world, social media can become a great source of tracking and being updated with the latest trends and lifestyle vogue.

Not only can entrepreneurs track the latest trends quantitatively using analytical tools like Google Trends, which reveal popular keywords among their target demography and their potential impact on digital advertising campaigns, but they can also glean insights by engaging directly with trendsetters. Empathizing with customers, observing their evolving needs, and understanding their journey can help startups accurately gauge lifestyle preferences and market trends in real time. By keeping a close eye on competitors, startups and businesses can also innovate new products and services based on the changing market needs, enabling them to be in sync with the changing environment and adapt to the current trends while surviving and thriving in the market.

For centuries, a single product cannot fulfill customers' needs throughout the year.

Even a gardener upgrades his garden with the relevant flowers and plants, keeping specific seasons in mind to make it look like a beautiful kaleidoscope of colors, textures, and foliage every time. Just like that, blooming a business requires pivoting the products every time a trend in the market changes.

From Decadence In Autumn To Rebirth In Spring.

Plants have their seasonal clock, which alters their structure, functioning, and growth based on seasonal changes. In spring, flowers bloom; in summer, fruits ripen; in autumn, leaves change color; and in winter, they fall and rest[4]. This process of plant's cyclical changes based on climatic changes is known as phenology.

However, plants do not have a calendar or a clock. All the changes they make to survive depend upon the external climatic conditions. Plants typically depend upon a specific set of triggers that helps them synchronize their growth and reproduction timings with favorable environmental conditions, which can range from triggers such as temperature (autumn and winter chilling and spring warming), photoperiod (length of day), precipitation, or, often, a combination of these. Plants change and adapt to changing climatic conditions to minimize the risk of damage they might have to bear if they do not adapt. Dormancy is one such mechanism in which plants have evolved over time to survive harsh climatic conditions. Not all plants survive all the changing weather conditions, probably because they haven't evolved enough to adapt to the changes.

Ever purchased marigolds for your garden? Do they survive after summer?

No. This is an example of a type of plant called annuals that only survive for one growing season, dying at the end of the summer or early fall[5]. Marigolds are plants whose whole plant, roots, stems, and leaves die, but they produce many seeds that sprout the following year, keeping the species alive.

The survival of big companies is also jeopardized when they do not adapt to the changing market trends. Without enough seeds spread across, their survival becomes near extinct. This happened in the Kodak company case, which failed because of its inability to pivot according to the changing market trends. When an organization or a business becomes too complacent with its idea, it forgets to adapt according to the customer's need, commencing its downfall. A significant shift was seen in people's lifestyles due to changing market trends with the emergence of digital cameras. However, due to its complacency, Kodak ignored user and customer feedback, wasting its time promoting film cameras instead of emulating its competitors[6]. The Kodak camera, which once was of premium quality and the first choice of professional photographers, declared bankruptcy in 2012 and eventually its demise.

Very evidently, the chilly and freezing winds of winter had surrounded this tree of Kodak. However, instead of shedding its leaves and adapting to the changing season, the tree stood still continuously, failing to adapt to the changing season, investing many resources in growing more fresh leaves and investing most of its funds in acquiring many small companies. Instead of depleting its money by branching out, it could have used the same to promote the sales of digital cameras, which were in demand, and by adapting to the changing market trends, it could have saved itself from hitting rock-bottom level.

Trees demonstrate remarkable adaptability by adjusting their internal anatomical structure and external physiology in response to changing seasons or environmental conditions.

Similarly, organizations must exhibit agility to thrive in dynamic market trends. Kodak's failure to adapt resulted in its inability to transition from the traditional camera era to the digital age. Instead of developing flexible strategies, the company relied on rigid approaches, leading to strategic challenges and missed opportunities.

Reinventing business over time is crucial for thriving in the market. Evolution and adaptation are critical to sustained success in the business world. It's not about merely having leaves and bearing fruits year-round; the accurate measure of success lies in consistently yielding fruits during the appropriate season, year after year, over the long term.

Companies that sense some disrupting forces affecting their industry more often divert sufficient resources to participate in emerging markets. It's just like the marigold plant, sensing the climate around it changing. So, it quickly starts spreading more and more seeds at diverse locations so that instead of becoming completely extinct, it gives birth to new plants, even if in the next season. Companies fail mainly because of their inability to truly embrace new business models, which emerge due to people's changing behaviors and lifestyles. In 1975, Steven Sasson of Eastman Kodak was the first engineer to develop the first digital camera[7]. He created a digital camera, invested in the technology, and even understood that photos could be shared online[8]. They failed to recognize that online photo sharing was the new business, not just a way of expanding their business by printing digital photos and keeping digital cameras with themselves instead of selling them.

The case study of Kodak is a classic lesson for all startups who feel that protecting their company's competitive advantage is essential. Instead, what is most important is to pivot according to the changing market trends and make radical and revolutionary changes. Even the tree takes time to grow fresh leaves, but once it does, it blooms more flowers and bears more fruits. Survival through agile adaptation has been the core of sustaining the business over the years.

A Crisis Can Be A Catalyst.

Plants not only survive and attempt to thrive in the changing climatic conditions, but they also develop ways of dealing with conditions that are not favorable for their growth, such as when the soil is too dry or too salty, most of them try to conserve their resources by growing fewer leaves and roots and by closing their open stomatal pores in order to hold water. Even though they take several adaptive measures, if the conditions remain harsh, many eventually die.

But, some plants are known as extremophiles (or extreme plants) because of their innovative evolution that has enabled them to handle harsh environments. *Schrenkiella parvula*, a scraggly, branching member of the mustard family, doesn't just survive in conditions that would kill most plants—it thrives in them. It grows along the shores of Lake Tuz in Turkey, where salt concentrations in the water can be six times higher than in the ocean[9].

Most plants show stunted growth when put in extreme and harsh conditions; however, harsh conditions are a green flag for these extremophiles to grow even more. These plants have a unique mechanism to combat the stresses of the environment. Researchers are studying these mechanisms to replicate them artificially in other plants and make their survival possible despite changing climatic conditions.

When plants encounter water-related stress in dry, salty, or cold conditions, they produce a hormone called abscisic acid, or ABA. This hormone activates specific genes that signal the plant to reduce its growth further, either by slowing or completely stopping it. However, the anomaly observed by the researchers was that while the other plants of the same Brassicaceae family show stunted growth, the roots of *Schrenkiella parvula* grow significantly faster under stressful conditions. This behavior is because, in *Schrenkiella parvula*, ABA activates different sections of its genetic code to create an entirely different behavior[10]. Thus, stressful conditions are not always growth inhibitors; they can be growth promoters, too. The crisis in the world functions the same way. They need not always be responsible for the failure of the startups or organizations but can be catalysts for their growth.

As we saw during the COVID-19 pandemic, it wreaked havoc on small, medium, and large businesses.

From seeing a crisis in the form of – the end of commuting, the collapse of brick and mortar, and the demise of travel and hospitality, we saw drastic growth in the number of startups that reinvented the entire hospitality and tourism industry, revolutionized the way people shop and completely transformed how people work and study. All this was possible because these companies considered the pandemic not as a roadblock but as a stepping stone to beget their growth.

As the companies reimagined their business model, they completely changed their outlook from just surviving to now thriving during the pandemic. For example, when working from home became the most prevalent norm, Zoom took over the usage as a verb instead of "to hoover or "to google[11]." People started using the term "Let's do Zoom" as the only means of working from home, and when Microsoft Teams and Google Meet also matched up their pace, zooming remained ubiquitous.

These companies could achieve this because they were SHAPEing their business suitably. The SHAPE that they gave to their business perspectives acted as a catalyst for growth during crisis[12]. SHAPE stands for –

S- Startup mindset: Instead of spending a majority of time researching, the companies adopted a startup mindset and began implementing innovations into action so that they could pilot test instead of analyzing based on research. This enabled them to pivot while they piloted their innovations. Connecting with the team for daily cadence calls and having a weekly review enabled the organizations to keep pace with the fast-changing trends.

H- Human at the core: The pandemic made the companies realize the importance of human life and well-being. Nothing became as valuable as human life and the need to be physically and mentally fit.

A- Acceleration of digital technology: It has already become a cliché: the COVID-19 crisis has accelerated the shift to digital. However, what worked best for the companies who pivoted their model and adapted to the new and changing trends was that they could enhance and expand their digital channels. By combining new data sources, such as satellite imaging, they could use advanced analytics successfully, not just for their insights, but to make better and faster decisions to strengthen the relationship with their customers.

P- Purpose-driven: Companies realized that the only way to survive is to switch from being profit-driven to being purpose-driven and offering what the customers need during a crisis. This further enabled them to dive deep into the customers' pain points and helped them innovate.

E- Ecosystems & adaptability: The pandemic brought a change not just at the modular level but at the ecosystem level. The startups realized that it wasn't enough to grow and sustain individually; instead, they needed to adapt to the changing world by altering the entire ecosystem through collaboration and cooperation.

These 5 parameters enabled the startups to grow during the pandemic. It accelerated the growth of those companies that could pivot their business models to remain relevant in the current world.

That's what organizations need to learn from plants and practice. Under extremely harsh drought conditions, they develop deep, long roots to ensure their survival over time through prolonged periods of drought. High winds and colds also pose a danger to trees' survival. But to survive these conditions, they either grow shallow to the ground or develop thick and full foliage that protects their trunk and stem from the wind, snow, and cold in the rainforests[13].

LIFESTYLE IS IN FLUX, NOTHING STAYS STILL

Food and fashion are the two most fluctuating industries where the choices and tastes of consumers can change overnight. These changing choices, preferences, and lifestyles of people influence business as well as their strategic decisions. Consumer habits and values are greatly influenced by the ever evolving demographic mix, cultural shifts, globalization as well as swift advancements in technology. Over time, these changes influence existing and emerging marketing trends and consumer lifestyles. Assimilating insightful knowledge about consumer preferences, choices, and tastes and constantly tracking their changing habits and values can be very beneficial for businesses to invest in emerging opportunities and scale up their ventures.

To stay relevant and competitive, startups and organizations must adapt their products to match evolving consumer behavior and emerging trends. This means pivoting their business models and innovating new products based on customer preferences, ensuring continued market relevance and sustainability.

Planting a coniferous tree in a desert will quickly wither and die if it is not suited to that environment. Even in hilly areas, these trees change to survive in different climates.

Similarly, adapting to customers' changing preferences and trends is crucial even if your target customers remain the same in business. Failing to adjust and pivot can lead to failure, even if you're targeting the same group of customers.

For example, let us consider the case of McDonald's, which initially began as a fast-food chain offering a combo of hamburgers and fries. McDonald's never offered salads or frappes initially. But to align with the changing tastes and transitioning lifestyle of diet-conscious people, it began offering healthier food options that the customers wanted, such as salads, frappes, fruits, wraps, oatmeals etc. It would have lost its importance if McDonald's had not responded to people's changing food choices.

What do you scout for when you go shopping? Do you search for the same style when buying new clothes?

No, because consumer's tastes often change with the changing fashion trends. We always prefer to look for new styles, so those in the fashion business must regularly innovate and update their inventories according to what their customers want.

The clothes a fashion business chooses to have in stock are also determined by what consumers want[14]. If consumers prefer to wear long dresses during one season, they would change their designs to suit their needs. Not only this, but they also have to keep themselves constantly on the go to suit the needs of the consumers based on the changing seasons. Boots and overcoats are needed in winter, which have no value during summer, and this fashion industry change should be not only adaptable to the consumer's choices but also agile based on the speed with which fashion changes with seasons.

Government policies and initiatives play a significant role in shaping how businesses respond to changing circumstances. Recently, there's been an emphasis on sustainability and eco-friendly practices. As a result, organizations and startups are adjusting their offerings to align with these trends, ensuring they don't harm the planet. For instance, a car cleaning company might promote its use of innovative, water-saving techniques to appeal to environmentally-conscious customers. These customers often pay a premium for products and services prioritizing sustainability.

Consumer behavior also influences how a service industry functions, not just product innovation. Consumer values and lifestyle are influenced by several factors ranging from impulsive buying behavior to brand perception, from fashion consciousness to health and fitness, from personal financial management to product innovativeness, and from family orientation to gender roles.

As a startup, there should be agility in innovating according to all these preferences. Nowadays, more than the product or the service, for customers, experience matters more. For example, people frequent 'hep' joints such as Barista and Starbucks not just to consume coffee but to savor the experience they get from the coffee's ambience, taste, and smell and often just for chit-chatting and enjoying.

Moreover, they do not mind paying that extra buck for all this[15].

The recent decade has seen the emergence of an era of Digital Darwinism, with players like Amazon.com, Gmail, Facebook, Instagram, and WhatsApp being the game changers for the new techie freak fashionable youth. The target segment for these companies has also changed from just the youth to the stylish professionals who are driven to prove their independence and have high aspirations and style statements. The combination of both these, service providers and the internet savvy worlds, can change the game's rules and set up a new world with more power to generate the flow of money in a quick manner[16].

At the core of every startup's agenda should be a commitment to align with shifting market trends, understand consumer behavior, and swiftly adapt to meet customer needs. Failure to do so can spell the gradual decline of the startup. As an entrepreneur, if you cannot innovate your product or service, ensure you sow the seeds of new ideas consistently. This way, even if one startup doesn't succeed, other ideas will be there to sprout and thrive.

With each changing season, plants alter their needs,

Be it the grass in the yard or the deciduous leaves.

Pivoting with changing trends is the only constant,

That is what every entrepreneur believes.

— Amya Madan

14.

STARTUPS AND RAINFORESTS

EMBRACING EFFECTIVENESS FOR SUCCESS

Efficiency is doing things right, and effectiveness is doing the right things.

– Peter Drucker

Efficiency & effectiveness – the two most used buzzwords in the corporate world!! They are often used interchangeably, but do they really mean the same? Not really.

These two terms have some stark differences, which are essential for all businesses and their stakeholders to understand and grasp. As an entrepreneur, do you ever ask yourself, "Can I be efficient without effectiveness? Or which is more important for the growth of my business— effectiveness or efficiency?

Let's turn to nature once again to uncover some insights. Why nature? Because it has a unique perspective on effectiveness and efficiency. While businesses and management often prioritize efficiency, nature emphasizes effectiveness above everything else.

Those organizations that value efficiency over effectiveness are those where the team's goal is to prioritize progress, success, and hitting targets with machine-like dedication regardless of whether they have enough resources or not[1]. No matter how limited the time or energy is, they are motivated by a methodical work process dominated by standardization and automation, focusing only on getting the maximum output.

The difference shows up in those organizations where, just like nature, the focus is on being more effective, i.e, investing their time, energy, and resources where the impact will be the most significant. Organizations require foresight to achieve effectiveness because they focus on the output and the journey toward that output. Effective team members are focused on doing the right things correctly. Though they too, are result-driven, their focus is more on achieving the bigger picture. A significant difference in an effective and efficient approach lies in the metric – for an effective team, quality matters over quantity, which is the opposite for an efficient team that values quantity over quality.

A simple example is of a team, which focuses on calling 200 clients daily to sell their insurance policy. Out of these 200 clients, if they can convert only 10% of clients because they focused more on reaching the target, then they are indeed efficient but ineffective.

On the other hand, if a team focuses on doing the proper market research, understanding their clients well before calling, and even if they can make only 70 calls in a day, but 50% of them buy their insurance, then that means they have very well stood on the effectiveness parameter. Those chasing targets follow a streamlined process to reach more prospective clients. However, effective people take different routes, paths, and creativity to achieve an impactful outcome. Nature has its way of illustrating that it is more effective than efficient.

Have you seen water flowing down from the mountain slope? Does that follow a straight path?

No, because instead of being efficient, it tries to be effective, carving its way through dry areas.

Similarly, a fly approaching a pot full of honey never follows a straight path but instead comes through a spiral pathway because of its unique compound eye construction. Think of any element in nature that tries to be effective instead of following an efficient straight line. The blood flowing in your veins, the helix structure of the DNA, and, for that matter, the seeds that disperse from one place to another are all examples of exceptional creativity and effectiveness portrayed by nature.

Have you heard about the phenomenon called "desierto florido" or flowering desert[2]? If not, this is a classic example of how nature transforms itself in unimaginable ways. This phenomenon occurs in the Atacama desert, one of the world's aridest deserts. But still, it blooms, though once in many years; this desert also supports life by converting into an umbrella of flowers that grow during years when there is exceptional rainfall. These flowers further give life to other small insects, birds, and lizards, creating an environment full of beauty and complexity. This example proves how nature functions in a manner that prioritizes effectiveness over efficiency, which sharply contrasts with what organizations in the current world have been focusing.

It is time to re-shift the focus from just chasing quantity over quality, productivity over impact. For startups to be successful, being efficient and getting many things done doesn't certainly mean increased productivity because even if there are more numbers, they might be doing the wrong tasks. Thus, for startups to succeed in the true sense, they must focus on becoming efficiently effective, which means using the right path to create a greater impact with the limited availability of resources.

Do the Right Things Well- Applying the 'Rainforest Principle'

Victor Hwang and Greg Horowitt, through their book "The Rainforest: The Secret to Building the Next Silicon Valley", uncovered various Rainforest principles that can be adopted and applied by startups to become creative and effective, just like rainforests are[3].

Over the centuries, rainforests have illustrated how seemingly lifeless and inorganic elements can be converted into organic matter, full of life. Since the Industrial Revolution, humans have tried to produce more and more, mainly at the cost of social, economic, and environmental impairment. Over the years, farmers have adopted various techniques to make farming productive and increase crop production, but at the cost of grave unintended consequences such as soil erosion, water scarcity, global warming etc. This is also true for the businesses and industries that have exploited natural resources to an extent that they can be called efficient but ineffective.

Now, it is time to be prudent and, while doing so, become effective. Organizations can learn from rainforests that have been magically supporting a diversity of life since humans didn't even exist. Rainforests have grown and thrived due to natural inputs like abundant rainfall, ideal temperature, appropriate moisture content, and dazzling sunlight. All these elements have been harmoniously working to inhabit diverse life forms in the rainforests. The marvels of the rainforest have been created not by the mere inventory of ingredients but rather by elusive magic.

Rainforests are a peculiar demonstration of the difference between organizations that function in a well-defined, orderly manner and those that exhibit creativity and an effective approach to thrive and grow. The world needs entrepreneurs who can apply the rainforest principle and become effective rather than just efficient.

Entrepreneurs need to be trailblazers to set an organization on a new trajectory. They should prioritize maximizing effectiveness over mere efficiency rather than trying to control every environmental factor. An analogy for this concept is how a farmer deals with weed growing in their field.

Some farmers selectively allow some variety of weed to grow on the field rather than plucking it off mercilessly. However, this requires foresight to identify which weed variety is edible and which needs to be protected. For example, dandelion is one of the most common and recognizable varieties of edible weeds, and it's also very versatile. The yellow petals from the dandelion flower and the leaves are eaten in salad, and the leaves can also be cooked and eaten – like spinach[4]. In the same fashion, entrepreneurs should also have the right skills to differentiate between harmful and harmless competitors so that instead of recklessly deploying resources to compete with them, they effectively find strategies to collaborate, merge, or acquire them.

For startups to grow, they should find ways where every stakeholder wins instead of devising strategies to win at the cost of someone losing. There is so much to learn from these rainforests, which, when applied to organizations, can blossom just like rainforests. Instead of accepting the way things are, creative entrepreneurs should challenge the status quo by overcoming it effectively. Those inspired by the rainforest principle, look at reality, but at the same time, they also have a vision to alter that reality for the betterment by looking at it freshly. A transformative vision is at the core of any successful startup which helps open up new horizons and paths to doing business. Transformation of the complete business industry can happen if the entrepreneurs work according to the principles of the rainforest. Deep within the soil, there are no resources and very few nutrients. According to this logic, rainforests would never be qualified for holding life. However, they are still home to millions of living species, plants, animals, microbes etc. They are more productive than any other business in the world, with a perfect blend of sustenance, complexity, and evolution. These environments excel by adapting to what they do not have[5].

In Japanese, there are two famous words: omote (the surface of an object or the external reality that one portrays) and ura (the underlying reality, the truth).

Remember studying about the rainforests?

The rainforest that we studied, full of dense, tall trees and diverse flora and fauna, was the omote. Now as an entrepreneur, it's time to get into the ura of these rainforests and take lessons from them to apply them in your venture and grow them as sustainable as these rainforests have been over several decades.

Rainforests follow a unique mechanism of sending positive and negative feedback, which leads to either a boost in their diversity or an increased level of deforestation. These feedback mechanisms ensure that homeostasis is maintained in the ecosystem. Tropical forests have maintained their diversity because of a negative feedback mechanism that ensures that the natural enemies (seed eater, herbivore, pathogen) keep populations in check. For example, consider an oak tree and a squirrel. The squirrel eats acorns and prefers to forage where oak trees are abundant. A squirrel isn't likely to notice a lone acorn in the middle of a grove of maples, whereas squirrels will eat many acorns in an oak grove. If this behavior is widespread in tropical rainforests, it could keep species from becoming too common[6].

Food webs are the most complex function in a rainforest. If a rainforest has to maintain a balance, it can only be achieved through dynamic equilibrium[7]. A famous French proverb says, "Plus ça change, plus c'est la même chose" (the more things change, the more they stay the same), which is very true for the rainforests.

Rainforests are those unique systems in nature that have survived for millions of years along the terrestrial zones of the equator. Despite being so complex, they have remained stable over the years, credit to their frantic feedback mechanism. Whenever a tree dies naturally, a gap in the soil sends positive feedback to the dormant sapling, which then starts growing. As new leaves are born, they capture the sunlight from the canopy of trees, leading to a higher rate of photosynthesis. This acts as the foundation for the emergence of new leaves. As more and more leaves grow, it can photosynthesize more, transforming the sapling into a mature tree. With each positive feedback that it gets, it grows exponentially.

But have you seen a tree growing forever?

No, because now the negative feedback mechanism pops up. When this negative feedback kicks in, it leads to a reduction in the growth rate of the tree. This limited growth is because of the phenomenon of evaporation that occurs internally within the tree. When the evaporation of water occurs through the stomata (pores) on the leaves, it creates a vacuum, which further sucks up more water from the soil through the tree. As the tree grows taller, the distance between the roots and the leaves increases, making the suction mechanism fragile. Thus, gradually, the tree stops growing taller.

Just like the rainforests maintain their equilibrium in diversity, organizations should maintain their balance while attracting diverse talent. While working on a startup, feedback mechanisms can indicate the potential for market demand. For example, if consumers favor a product, greater demand is created, creating a gap that has to be filled by the supply of more products. When the companies avoid harming the environment, an alert is sent to the company to continue making products, which, in turn, earns them profit. For example, Mitsubishi developed one of the first refrigerators that did not use chlorofluorocarbons- the chemical responsible for eating away the ozone layer- and is now a leader in that market[5] .

Diversity is integral to any rainforest because if two species have the same niche, then according to the law of "survival of the fittest," only one will survive. That is why the species in a rainforest have adopted a simple principle of nonconformity: conformity leads to extinction. This same principle applies to the business world. One will likely fail if two companies are too similar, targeting the same customers with the same technology.

Companies must offer something unique that distinguishes them from the competition to thrive.

Diversity in organizations is indispensable for the expansion of the business. If two companies make exactly the same leading-edge product, only one survives. One must compromise on the product, service, or profits to sustain.

Do you think that happens in the rainforest?

No, because in a rainforest ecosystem, there are no losers but many winners. Each organism gets a chance to win through diversity and its uniqueness. This can be true for businesses as well. However, to achieve that, they should not focus on fitting themselves into solving social problems but on fulfilling a social problem in the best possible manner; while doing so, they will survive and excel. Currently, most companies are curtailing their costs markedly in a rush to seek the lowest price game. But this isn't a more innovative way to differentiate. In order to excel, they need to create distinctive products that cater to fulfilling the needs of unique niches, not all. Not all organizations can keep competing, trying to sell the cheapest product at the cost of value and quality. If they do so, either their competitors will crush them, or they will crush others. The only way to survive and excel in this regard is to create unique, high-quality products that ensure a good user experience for the customers. That means startups and businesses today are required to become unique, diverse, and distinctive from others, not in terms of price but more in terms of value. So, instead of volume, they should focus more on value.

Diversity plays a vital role both externally and internally within the organization. Internally, diversity needs to be backed by partnerships, which is evident in how a rainforest sustains innumerable life forms that coexist harmoniously. Startups and organizations can ensure this sustainability through internal diversity by attracting and managing the right talent. In the book, 'How Kiran Mazumdar Shaw fermented Biocon,' Kiran Shaw talks about how dogmatic she is in her desire to attract and retain the best talent. She states, and I quote, "One of my strengths is choosing people. I always look for those who are more competent than me. Having a more competent team is no reason to feel insecure because each one has their own strength and each strength is important[8]."

This is in corroboration to how the rainforests have been able to burgeon in diversity.

All the people in an organization with different, unique talents and abilities provide a new perspective to the organization. The novel perspectives make the organization more creative as well as resilient. Diversity improves performance, creates positive friction that enhances deliberation, and upends conformity[9].

A diverse team enables entrepreneurs to connect the dots and intersect parallels within the unparallel industries more facilely. In the words of Charles Bark (Founder and CEO, HiNounou), "Diversity is not an option, but a must. Diversity is a huge richness – especially for a startup that has the vision to go worldwide and impact the lives of people on all continents[10]."

However, diversity might sometimes make people in an organization uneasy and frictionless.

Imagine a rainforest where there are no earthworms, no eagles, or no plants. Will the food web ever be complete? No, because for each of these diverse organisms to co-exist, they must be included in the same ecosystem, interdependence, and partnerships to survive. Similar is the case with organizations, so entrepreneurs should also focus on inclusion and diversity. Padma Vibhushan, Dr. R.A. Mashelkar, says and I quote, "India needs growth, but more importantly, it needs inclusive growth, where no Indian is left behind. India's progress should prioritize inclusive growth, which entails to providing education, conducting research, and fostering innovation to develop products and services accessible to all, not just the privileged few. Therefore, businesses must not only unite their diverse team members under a shared vision but also innovate in ways that benefit everyone, regardless of their background or status[11]."

Nature, particularly rainforests, offers valuable inspiration for businesses and startups. Yet, to derive insights and ideas from nature, entrepreneurs must adopt a unique perspective and strive to craft innovative and original solutions.

Have you ever seen the petals of a lotus flower dirty?

There was an individual who didn't merely move on upon capturing stunning images of lotus flowers. Intrigued by the lotus petal's unique trait of repelling dirt and algae, he researched its mechanism more deeply. The lotus leaf's surface possesses microscopic bumps that prevent water molecules from sticking, enabling rainwater to wash away debris effortlessly[12]. Inspired by such natural phenomena, great entrepreneurs and innovators don't settle for observation; they seek answers to their curious inquiries.

They apply learnings from natural phenomena to create marvels in the business world. A German company called ISPO, after observing this "Lotus effect," came up with a new product called the Lotusan[13]. Lotusan is an environmentally friendly house paint that utilizes a microstructure formula inspired by the hydrophobic leaves of the lotus plant. This innovative approach minimizes the contact area between water and dirt, resulting in a wall paint that stays remarkably clean and free from dirt. Drawing inspiration from nature involves more than just observing its static form; observing nature in motion is essential. Innovators are increasingly leveraging observations of plant movements to create impactful designs and solutions. The Mimosa plant, popularly known as the touch-me-not plant, shows movement due to the altering concentration of water on its surface, which sends signals to the cells to either collapse or expand. At the University of Michigan, researchers are trying to replicate the remarkable motion of the Mimosa plant. They aim to develop adaptive structures that can mimic this plant's movement. They're exploring innovative technology resembling snake-like robots capable of maneuvering through tunnels and then transitioning to a rigid state to grip objects. This transformation would occur autonomously, triggered solely by changes in hydraulic pressure, eliminating the need for manual or computerized cues. Additionally, they envision aircraft with flexible wings similar to birds, capable of adjusting their wing shape to suit changing flight conditions[14]. Envisioning such ideas inspired by the plants is the first step toward building a sustainable economy.

Remember those childhood days when children frequently endeavored to replicate tree structures while constructing their own clubhouses and engaging in imaginative play beneath the branches? Climbing trees and utilizing various elements, they constructed distinctive and innovative structures. Little did they know, they were already displaying entrepreneurial traits, inadvertently crafting their own wonders inspired by the tree.

Not just that, the tree has been a recurrent source of inspiration for designers across the globe, from Japanese practitioners such as Sou Fujimoto to Burkina Faso's maverick architect Francis Kéré[15]. An example of this tree-inspired structure is constructed in Kuala Lumpur's Ilham Gallery which is an innovative bio-inspired design and is a permanent home built according to the tropical Malaysian climes[16]. Rainforests are true marvels that can serve as blueprints for businesses and startups across all sectors. Within their vast expanse lies a plethora of lessons waiting to be explored. Whether it's about fostering partnerships, embracing collaboration, or cultivating uniqueness while maintaining diversity, nature offers invaluable insights. By observing and adjusting the lens through which we view plants and their structures, astonishing designs and architectures can be constructed.

The principles of the rainforest have the power to transform how businesses operate completely. While doing so, entrepreneurs can harness the benefits of the diverse flora and fauna in the form of their pool of talented employees, much like how nature does.

In today's ever-changing, volatile, uncertain, and ambiguous business landscape, entrepreneurs must shift their mindset away from mechanical, linear thinking and toward a more biological mindset This means prioritizing effectiveness over efficiency, adapting to the environment, and thriving amidst uncertainty.

Gaze at those plants blooming in the rainforest,

Oh! What a creation, makes us feel so blest.

Learn from them, over volume, how to prioritize value

Effectiveness, they call it, apply now...shall you?

– Amya Madan

15.

INCENTIVIZING INNOVATION
THE BEE-NECTAR WAY

"The reward for work well done is the opportunity to do more"

– Jonas Sulk

In the initial years of their journey, startups are primarily engrossed in product development, market expansion, and team building. However, during this phase, there is often a neglect of maximizing value creation—such as ensuring swifter delivery, superior quality, and competitive pricing. As startups progress and evolve, they realize that stagnation has set in despite their market expansion efforts. In any startup's trajectory, stagnation is a concerning indicator of growth impediment.

Nature works according to the fundamental law of survival, where every living organism, including plants, has an innate drive to eat, drink, sleep, and reproduce. Procreation is vital for their growth and the continuity of their species. Unlike animals, plants are rooted in one place, unable to move around to spread their seeds and reproduce.

So, how do they manage to expand their presence globally?

They do so by dispersing their seeds through various channels such as water, air, or, at times, by sticking to animal bodies. On top of all these channels, plants take the bees' help or use other pollinators to work for them. These bees become helping hand for the flowers by carrying their pollen grains from one flower to another. Bees are crucial because pollen grains of some flowers are heavy, making them difficult to be carried away by the wind. That is why flowers need bees!

Doesn't it sound like a startup that recruits a team of employees and interns to promote its brand to customers and grow the business? This process mirrors the concept of pollination, where the startup founder, sitting in one place, cannot grow the business alone. Much like a plant, he/she needs a team to collaborate and help reach out to customers globally.

But nobody works for free! Even nature rewards bees for their hard work with nectar. Similarly, startups need to motivate and reward their team for their efforts.

Over the years, nature has understood the importance of motivating and rewarding bees and pollinators. Plants reward these pollinators who aid them in spreading their seeds and pollen grains in the form of nectar or oils and sometimes with fragrant smells and pheromones to attract them. Even the tiniest creatures, like bees, deserve rewards for their hard work! So do the humans who expect acknowledgment and rewards for their efforts.

A beautiful symbiotic relationship exists between bees and flowers, where each is naturally drawn to the other, showcasing the power of mutual appreciation and support in nature. Flowers release pheromones and chemicals to help bees find the flowers containing the nectar they need. Unknowingly, bees, which land on the plants to feed on the nectar, carry pollen grains. When they move to other flowers, they inadvertently spread these grains, aiding in pollination and the growth of new flowers.

A similar relationship exists between employees looking for a job and the startup founders. Think of startups as flowers and employees as bees. Just as flowers need bees to spread pollen and grow, startups need employees to expand their business and succeed. Just like bees, employees are selective. They're attracted to startups that offer them rewards like good pay and good career growth opportunities.

Similarly, bees are not attracted to all flowers; they only land on a flower if they get the desired rewards in the form of nectar and pollen grains.

Incentives and rewards also act as powerful management tools for startups as well. Just as bees need nectar to pollinate flowers, employees need rewards to innovate. It's a give-and-take relationship: employees come up with fresh ideas, and in return, they receive recognition, bonuses, or other perks – paid leaves, holiday trips, appreciation, etc., that keep them motivated to continue working towards achieving the company's vision.

Just as bees transfer pollen from one flower to another, sparking new growth, innovation thrives when ideas from one department influence another. Startups need fresh perspectives to grow, but founders alone can't do it all. They rely on creative minds to bring new ideas to the table. To keep these innovators buzzing, startups must offer rewards, like nectar to bees, in the form of good pay and fringe benefits to attract and retain top talent who can drive innovation.

In nature, bees innately gravitate towards flowers that offer them abundant nectar and enticing scents. They instinctively keep visiting these flowers for sustenance. However, if they find that a flower lacks nectar, they gradually stop visiting it and seek out other flowers. Similarly, in organizations, motivated employees thrive when they are rewarded for their innovation. They go the extra mile to generate fresh ideas. But if they feel their efforts are not adequately recognized or rewarded, they may consider moving on to other opportunities. Just as every flower is unique, each startup has its own culture and practices. What motivates employees in one startup may not necessarily work for those in another. Therefore, while rewarding innovation is essential for employee motivation, startups must also be mindful of how and what they reward to ensure continued success.

Let's consider a bulb-manufacturing company called XYZ Pvt. Ltd. They struggled to meet their monthly production targets, leading to decreased profits due to delayed orders. Taking a cue from nature, the company introduced an incentive program: Employees who reach their monthly targets would receive a 20% bonus and a trip to Bangkok. Motivated by the promise of rewards, employees worked harder and exceeded their targets by the month's end. The incentive program seemed triumphant as the company achieved its goals and treated employees to a trip. However, upon their return, customers complained about the poor quality of the bulbs. This raised a critical question: Did the company reward the right behavior? The rush to meet production targets led employees to prioritize quantity over quality, driven solely by the desire for the promised trip. While incentives are essential, startups must carefully consider which behaviors they reward to avoid unintended consequences.

Plants reward pollinators with a diverse variety of resources. While nectar is most talked about, many plants instead reward bees with protein-rich pollen, fragrant oils, or resins[1]. Thus, while designing any incentive scheme or reward system for their startup, entrepreneurs should look at it from a broader perspective and test which reward works best for them. Apart from the conventional reward systems such as bonuses or paid holidays or trips, there are novel rewards which can act as nectars for the employees. The **FRAP framework** can help achieve this.

Frap is a term that simply means to hold or bind something together. Applying this terminology in the work culture can help the organization keep employees committed and connected to them through a strong bond, preventing them from finding a different flower (a new company).

FRAP is an abbreviation for

F- Freedom & Flexibility

R- Recognition & appreciation

A- Acceptance of ideas

P- Prize & Promotion

Freedom plays a vital role in shaping human behavior and fostering creativity. In a constrained environment, individuals often experience stress and struggle to generate new ideas. Recognizing this, startups should prioritize allowing employees to explore and experiment. Rewarding their efforts, even in the face of failure, is essential for fostering innovation. Cultivating a culture of free thought and expression across all levels of the organization encourages the development of new ideas.

Moreover, promoting flexibility in working hours and roles is a valuable reward for innovative contributions. If flexible working isn't something you already do, it's time to get started[2]. This would incentivize creativity and enhance employee satisfaction and overall productivity.

Recognition serves as a powerful reward mechanism, often following a task's completion or an initiative's successful outcome. By acknowledging and appreciating employee efforts, organizations can foster a positive workplace environment and cultivate a sense of belongingness among their workforce. When innovative ideas are recognized, individuals feel incentivized to think creatively, knowing their contributions will be valued.

This aligns with Maslow's hierarchy of needs, highlighting the human desire for love and belongingness, which can be fulfilled in the workplace through recognition and appreciation. Moreover, recognition promotes growth and change within the company by instilling a sense of security among employees, reaffirming their value to the organization, and motivating them to continue their exemplary work.

Acceptance of ideas, though challenging at times, serves as a consistent motivator for employees to continue generating innovative concepts. While not every idea may evolve into a major project, generating even one idea can be a significant achievement for an employee. Organizations have the opportunity to foster a culture of acceptance by embracing employee ideas as valuable contributions to the company's growth. Rather than outrightly rejecting or dismissing ideas, organizations can accept them as genuine efforts and offer guidance and mentorship to refine and develop them. By practicing this approach, organizations can encourage a continuous flow of creative and innovative ideas within the company, contributing to its overall success and evolution.

Prizes and promotions are tangible rewards that can effectively motivate employees to generate innovative ideas. While the previous rewards primarily address the psychological aspects of motivation, tangible rewards give employees something concrete in return for their efforts. Offering prizes, gift hampers, awards, and other tangible incentives can be an impactful way to recognize and reward organizational innovation.

Additionally, promotions based on individual contributions further acknowledge employees' dedication and commitment to the company. These promotions offer monetary rewards and elevate employees' status within the organization, serving as a significant motivator to maintain their commitment and drive.

THE SECRET SIGNALS THAT GUIDE BEES' NAVIGATION

How do bees know which flowers to go onto without knowing their quality or quantity of nectar?

Not all flowers can provide a good amount of nectar to the bees, but still, they need them for pollination. They attract bees through their floral traits and characteristics. Some flowers modify their shape, size, or color.

In contrast, some other flowers secrete chemical scents or even produce electric fields and movements, which help the pollinators recognize and get attracted to them. Floral colors are essential characteristics for pollinators when deciding which flower to choose. However, how bees perceive the flowers' colors differs significantly from how humans look at colors[3]. The flower's color also varies with age and might become dark or light depending on its growth. Different pollinators pollinate on the same flower depending on their unique color preferences. For example, *Quisqualis indica* tends to change its flower color from white to pink to red, known as a change from moth to butterfly pollination. Firstly, the hawkmoths pollinate the flowers that blossom in white, and when the flowers turn pink and eventually red, they droop and are pollinated by bees, flies, and other possible insects[4]. That is why flowers are the most attractive part of the plant; through this part, they can attract the best pollinators for pollination. The shape and size of a flower also play an equal role in attracting pollinators to the flower.

Over the years, flowers have evolved their shape and size in order to become the most suitable for what pollinators are attracted to. A positive connection exists between the size of flowers, inflorescences, or flower fields and attractiveness to insects. The smaller flowers or inflorescences are thought to suffer lower visitation rates due to the insect's incompetence in detecting them[5]. The larger the flower, the more successful it is in attracting pollinators towards it.

HEADING TOWARDS THE FINAL MILESTONES

While discussing the Innovation model at the beginning of this book, we established the analogy of the flowers as the break-even point for a startup. After going through different stages of growth, maturity, and change, the seed growing in the soil gives rise to flowers, the most beautiful ornament to the glory of a plant.

Just like a seed, an entrepreneur faces numerous obstacles and triumphs while reaching the break-even milestone. This pivotal moment marks a significant achievement for the entrepreneur, signaling readiness to reap the rewards of his hard work and dedication. Upon reaching the break-even stage, the entrepreneur experiences a sense of accomplishment and anticipation as their startup is poised to generate profits and make a meaningful impact. At this juncture, the revenue the company generates becomes sufficient to cover its operating expenses i.e., reaches its break-even. Moreover, achieving break-even status enhances the startup's appeal to top talent, as it can now offer competitive compensation packages. This, in turn, attracts skilled professionals who contribute innovative ideas and expertise, further fueling the startup's growth trajectory.

Like flowers attract more pollinators when they bloom into larger, more vibrant blossoms, startups that reach their break-even point become magnets for talent. This milestone signifies the startup's maturity and success, analogous to a seed's transformation into a beautiful flower. As the startup establishes itself as a prominent player in the market, it gains recognition and prestige, drawing in a larger pool of applicants eager to join its team. Like flowers attract pollinators to spread their pollen grains, the startup which has reached break-even, attracts top talent seeking to be part of its burgeoning journey. Talented and creative job seekers often overlook startups that are yet to turn profitable or lack visibility in the market. Instead, they are attracted to financially stable and prosperous companies, offering them a promising environment to apply their skills. However, this does not mean smaller flowers cannot attract pollinators or grow. Nature has its solutions to overcome limitations and continue thriving. Plants with inconspicuous flowers have developed unique strategies to attract pollinators. They gather together into large clusters, called inflorescences, to enhance their visibility and attract pollinators. Similarly, startups can employ innovative strategies to attract top talent and grow their teams, even if they are not profitable or widely recognized[6].

The same can be learned and adopted by small-scale startups as well. By collaborating and partnering with several other businesses in their industry, these startups can bloom into big ventures, attracting more competent people. Apart from the flowers' color, size, and shape, they also use some olfactory signals to attract pollinators. These olfactory signals in the form of fragrance or scent enable the flowers to attract bees searching for nectar.

WHAT DO YOU THINK THESE OLFACTORY SIGNALS WOULD BE FOR A STARTUP?

Very simple. It is the advertising and the appropriate branding of the startup. Like flowers release fragrances to attract pollinators, startups can use digital marketing and other advertisements to signal job opportunities and entice potential candidates. These signals act as effective communication channels, inviting skilled individuals to join the startup, contribute to innovation, and be rewarded for their efforts, much like bees are drawn to flowers by their enticing scents.

While flowers that birds pollinate are usually scentless, flowers pollinated by insects often emit fragrance. At night, it is difficult for pollinators to trace flowers because of low visibility, which causes the visual cues to go for a toss. That is why night-blooming plants emit strong, penetrating floral scents necessary for long-distance. In day-blooming plants, however, the floral scents are not as strong as they are visible to the pollinators, so they focus more on modifying their structure, appearance, and color to attract their pollinators. Similarly, to increase the visibility of the startup, long-lead advertisements are a must to reach the right people.

CAREFUL! THE FLORAL ATTRACTION MIGHT BE DECEIT.

Not all flowers follow genuine mechanisms to attract pollinators. They don't modify their color or shape or secrete any olfactory chemicals to attract the bees toward them. Instead, mimicry is a common pollination strategy that they use. With mimicry, these flowers don't offer pollination rewards like pollen or nectar. Instead, they deceive pollinators into visiting them, using tactics that mimic the appearance or behavior of flowers that offer rewards. For instance, in begonia, only male flowers provide pollen rewards[7]. The end goal of this adaptation is to attract pollinators in order to mature and spread through pollination.

Employees must be cautious not to fall into the trap of startups that might deceive them with false claims. Like deceptive flowers, startup founders can advertise their ventures as unicorns or claim to have reached break-even status, attracting potential employees through social media platforms.

Don't get swayed away so quickly, just like those bees and the insects. They don't have a fully developed brain and central nervous system. But you have one! Before rushing into any decision, take a moment to consider and thoroughly research the veracity of the information provided by a startup before believing it. Look into the company's actual growth and whether they genuinely reward innovation in the workplace. Many startups boast about incentive schemes, but few follow through, much like flowers that attract pollinators without offering any nectar in return. Therefore, verifying all claims before applying to any startup or company is essential. And if you discover that a company doesn't fulfill its promises, don't hesitate to seek opportunities elsewhere!

Through this fascinating interaction between pollinators and plants, it's clear that pollinators such as bees are drawn to plants that offer them nectar. Similarly, startups can attract talented individuals and foster innovation through the FRAP mechanism, leading to rapid growth. Just as pollinators revisit flowers that offer them more significant rewards, rewarding innovation and embracing employee ideas can enhance loyalty and retention within a startup, thus creating a sense of security for employees and fueling long-term growth and expansion.

Drenched in fresh dew, a flower needs a bee

To feed on its nectar, carrying its pollen beyond the sea.

Your employees need rewards to continue innovation,

Motivate them by giving lots of rewards and appreciation.

– Amya Madan

Conclusion

Entrepreneurship is a journey of challenges, triumphs, and endless growth opportunities. As we come to the final chapter of our journey—a journey that has taken us from a tiny seed to the transformative impact of entrepreneurship, let's reflect on the lessons learned and the insights gained.

In the beginning, we planted the seed of an idea—an idea that, much like a seed, holds within it the potential to grow, evolve, and change the world. Just as a seed requires nourishment and care to sprout, so does an idea, that needs nurturing and encouragement to take root and flourish. We learned that every great accomplishment starts with a small idea, and it is up to us how much we cultivate and nurture those ideas into something impactful. But, as much as the quality of the seed is important, so is the importance of an idea that holds the potential to create a huge impact. To understand this better, we conducted thorough market research, gathered customer feedback, and stayed attuned to industry trends, so that we could sow our seeds in well-prepared soil i.e make data-driven decisions for growing our idea in the right market.

In the words of Winston Churchill, *"Success is not final, failure is not fatal; It is the courage to continue that counts."* As we nurtured our ideas, we encountered challenges and setbacks along the way. But just as a seedling bends but does not break in the wind, so too must we persevere in the face of adversity. We learned that resilience is the key to success and that every obstacle we overcome brings us one step closer to achieving our goals. Just like trees protected themselves from strong winds, we safeguarded our ventures from external threats and market forces by protecting intellectual property rights and ensuring strong governance practices. By prioritizing IPR protection and implementing robust governance frameworks, entrepreneurs can mitigate risks and build a foundation for sustainable growth.

With time and perseverance, our ideas began to take shape, growing and evolving into something magnificent. Like a tree that reaches toward the sky, our ventures reached new heights, leaving a lasting impact on the world around us. But this wouldn't have been possible without seeking guidance from experienced mentors and industry veterans who gave valuable insights to avoid common pitfalls and accelerate our path to success. Moreover, for taking our ventures to new heights, access to capital from diverse funding sources and investors helped fuel growth and scaling operations.

While nourishing our ideas, we celebrated the power of innovation to drive positive change. Innovation is the lifeblood of entrepreneurship which allows entrepreneurs to stay ahead of the curve and create value in a rapidly evolving marketplace by continuously iterating and refining ideas through creativity and out-of-the-box thinking.

Over the course of this book, we've also learned that collaboration is the cornerstone of innovation and growth. By fostering partnerships and leveraging mentorship, entrepreneurs can overcome challenges and unlock new opportunities. However, while doing so it's important to remember that in the ever-changing world of business, risk management is paramount. By carefully assessing risks and implementing strategic safeguards, entrepreneurs can navigate uncertainty and safeguard their ventures against potential pitfalls.

As our tree began to branch out and become stronger, we found that each anatomical plant part plays an essential role in nurturing and strengthening it. Each tissue has a significant and critical role to play. Thus, for startups, building a cohesive and motivated team is essential for success. By fostering a culture of trust, communication, and collaboration, entrepreneurs can harness the collective talents and strengths of their team to drive innovation and achieve shared goals. But to foster a positive and productive work environment, they should recognize and reward the contributions of employees by incentivizing innovation and providing opportunities for growth and development. Doing this would cultivate a loyal and motivated workforce – a workforce that is diverse yet inclusive. Entrepreneurs can tap into a wealth of perspectives and experiences by leveraging a diverse and inclusive workplace.

As the book draws to a close, let us remember that the journey from seed to impact is not just a destination—it is a testament to the resilience of the human spirit and the boundless potential of the human mind. Let us go forth with courage, conviction, and an unwavering belief in the transformative power of ideas. May we never cease to be inspired by the awe-inspiring beauty and wisdom of the natural world that continues to guide and inspire us on our entrepreneurial journey.

Ultimately, it is not just about planting seeds or nurturing ideas—it is about harnessing the power of imagination, innovation, and collaboration to create a brighter, more sustainable future for all.

Thank you for joining me on this remarkable journey. May your seeds of innovative ideas take root, flourish, and bear fruits, leaving an enduring legacy of impact and inspiration for generations to come.

Bonus Chapter

Building Resilience through PARADOS Strategy

Sustaining businesses over time also requires resilience, to try again one more time when failed. While writing this book and understanding the importance of resilience, I was able to coin a new concept called the **"PARADOS strategy,"** which can enable businesses to practice resilience over time.

During the war, soldiers build parados that provide protection and defense from the rear. This structure supports the trench, providing constant support, safety, and the ability to fight back during unforeseen situations. Likewise, resilience is necessary within an organisation when faced with disruptive environmental conditions, economic slowdowns, or emerging competition and threats.

The survival and success of the business depend upon the *PARADOS strategy*, which, in my words, is an acronym for

P- Prudence

A- Autonomy

R- Repurposing

A- Agile adaptability

D- Decentralization

O- Objectivity

S- Symbiotic interaction.

Let us take the example of the human immune system to understand further how we can implement the Parados strategy. Our body fights innumerable bacteria, viruses, and other pathogens without our knowledge. The immune system detects anomalies or threats to our system and responds immediately. This defense works through local response and interaction to protect a global system. In addition, once attacked by a specific pathogen, the immune system can memorize this pattern and learn its responses, providing better protection when faced with the same threat again. These memory cells reactivate and trigger a response. Some astounding properties of the immune system are its resilience, autonomy, decentralization, memory retention, and recognition. These factors can enormously increase efficiency, growth, and success when applied to organizations.

Prudence: In the same way that the immune system is always on alert and prepared, organizations should adopt this characteristic better to prepare their workforce for uncertain or unforeseen situations. By plausibly envisioning the negative scenarios, organizations can prepare mind maps for mitigating risks. Doing this will help combat threats from competitors or other threatening factors.

Autonomy: The cells in the immune system are autonomous and work under no management, yet belong to a single system. In organizations, the hierarchy of people is essential, but independent decision-making is the key to staying resilient. Self-organization enables the immune system cells to determine their unique ways of detecting a threat and then taking a proper course of action, providing the immune system with the distinctive feature of quickly selecting and reacting to the attack.

Similarly, assuming that everyone in an organization is self-organized and autonomous, it is easier to defend the threat from various possible sources, which leads to a quicker response rate than waiting for the situation to hop from one hierarchy to another. However, autonomy brings the massive responsibility of ensuring that the response to the threat is appropriate; only then can it be fought. If any cell in the immune system finds itself incapable of dealing with a threat, it ensures alerting its neighboring cells. Thus, in organizations, if an employee or team cannot deal with a specific situation autonomously, they should

immediately ask for support.

Re-purposing: This attribute refers to creating a backup plan if the first action fails. As in the case of the immune system, multiple copies of a single antibody exist, allowing the body to deal with the pathogen more efficiently. The numerous copies also ensure that even if one antibody fails to match with the antigen, there will be another one to destroy it. Precisely, organizations should follow this strategy. They should train their employees to be versatile so that in case of emergencies, there is always somebody equipped to handle these situations.

Agile Adaptability: Agility refers to the quickness of the immune system's response rate. If there was any delay in the reaction time of the immune cells, it could lead to the antigen entering the body and causing harm. So, agility is equally vital as adaptability. Adaptability ensures that the immune cells can recognize the new pathogens and, at the same time, also devise new ways of responding. This adaptation mechanism allows it to adjust to new and changing environmental conditions internally and externally.

Similarly, organizations should have a system where a solution gets applied immediately as and when the threat shows up. It is essential to establish an adaptable mechanism that the company consistently adheres to, ensuring that any shifts in the external environment or internal conflicts do not adversely affect the organization's overall functioning.

Decentralization: This is one of the most significant and unique features of the immune system, wherein no single organ or cell is responsible for identifying foreign attackers. Thus, the body will hold no single unit responsible for the immune system's failure.

Similarly, organizations should decentralize their departments, providing enough autonomy and freedom to different departments. Doing so allows for a quicker response rate and helps avoid the blame game in inefficient organizations. Organizations can avoid this by formulating a multi-agent approach.

Objectivity (Purpose-driven): Along with the freedom to subjectively interpret a situation, the employees in an organization should possess some degree of objectivity, enabling them to drive their functions more purposefully. While every cell in the body can counterattack and respond to a threat, not all cells launch a collective counter-attack against the pathogen. Such a unified response would be inefficient and wasteful in terms of energy and resources.

To circumvent this, only the cells in the specific region where the pathogen attempts to invade become activated. The immune system precisely operates as each cell and organ comprehends its designated purpose and function. For organizations to succeed, they should draw on this to define the roles and responsibilities of all of their employees objectively and coherently so that the employees have a sense of purpose and are confident about when to act and when not to. It also ensures that the company does not exhaust all its resources while addressing a threat or challenge.

Symbiotic Interaction: The cells in the immune system are autonomous yet synchronized because they exhibit "symbiosis." Many cells in the immune system co-exist by performing diverse functions yet interacting with each other in a highly coordinated and mutually beneficial manner. Not all cells are involved in immune response; instead, some are responsible for memorizing the pathogens, some inhibit the growth of the pathogen, while others are involved in the renewal of the ruptured cells within the body.

Additionally, the pathogen has to pass through multiple layers of defense set up by the immune system before it can attack the host body. These numerous layers function in a highly symbiotic manner to provide maximum protection to the body.

Similarly, organizations can only succeed and thrive when all their diverse departments have a symbiotic relationship. For example, organizations cannot hire employees without a human resources department or process their salary without a finance and audits department. Organizations can only earn this revenue to pay salaries to the operations department, and the operations department can only perform well if there is a stellar product development department with an efficient marketing and sales unit. This entire interaction denotes why symbiotic interaction is crucial in an organization as much as it is in the proper functioning of our immune system. Combining all these facets of the growth of a seed into a tree demonstrates why protecting businesses from competition is crucial to the success of an "En-tree-preneur."

Notes

Part 1- Sowing Seeds = Seeding Ideas

Chapter 1 - Nascence: Sowing the Seeds of an Idea

1. https://precisionagricultu.re/selecting-the-best-seeds-for-your-farm/#:~:text=Examining%20the%20ground%20can%20help,to%20choose%20the%20best%20seeds.

2. https://hasanuzzaman.weebly.com/uploads/9/3/4/0/934025/seed_quality.pdf

3. https://www.woodlandtrust.org.uk/blog/2020/12/what-is-a-seed-bank/#:~:text=A%20seed%20bank%20is%20a,%2D%20around%20%2D20%20%C2%B0C.

4. https://vikaspedia.in/agriculture/agri-inputs/seeds/seed-quality

5. https://knowledge.wharton.upenn.edu/article/the-inside-story-behind-the-unlikely-rise-of-airbnb/

6. https://en.wikipedia.org/wiki/SCAMPER#:~:text=SCAMPER%20was%20proposed%20by%20Alex,SCAMPER%3A%20Games%20for%20Imagination%20Development.

7. https://vestinadesign.wordpress.com/2020/03/13/mcdonalds-history-and-scamper-method/

8. http://www.syque.com/quality_tools/tools/Tools102.htm#:~:text=This%20is%20where%20the%20PINC,developed%20into%20more%20useful%20solutions.

9. https://agriculturistmusa.com/importance-of-seeds/

10. https://inc42.com/features/indias-unicorn-club-the-comprehensive-list-of-unicorns-in-india/

11. https://krishijagran.com/agripedia/5-probable-reasons-your-seeds-fail-to-germinate/

12. https://www.failory.com/blog/Startup-failure-rate

13. https://www.embroker.com/blog/Startup-statistics/#:~:text=About%2090%25%20of%20Startups%20fail.&text=10%25%20of%20Startups%20fail%20within%20the%20first%20year.&text=Across%20all%20industries%2C%20Startup%20failure,be%20close%20to%20the%20same.&text=Failure%20is%20most%20common%20for,70%25%20falling%20into%20this%20category.

14. https://www.cbinsights.com/research/Startup-failure-reasons-top/

15. https://www.researchgate.net/publication/325011454_Why_Do_Startups_Fail_A_Case_Study_Based_Empirical_Analysis_in_Bangalore/link/5af15e610f7e9ba366456773/download

16. Gartner, W., Starr, J. and Bhat, S. (1999) Predicting new venture survival: an analysis of 'anatomy of a start-up', cases from Inc. magazine, Journal of Business Venturing, 14(2), 215-232.

17. Chorev, S. and Anderson, A.R. (2006) Success in Israeli high-tech start-ups; critical factors and process, Technovation, 26(2), 162-174.

Chapter 2 - Entrepreneurial Mindset: Unearthing Farmer's Traits

1. https://www.grainsa.co.za/love,-hard-work-and-character-make-the-farmer

2. Abdullah F. et al (2009), Developing a framework of success of Bumiputera entrepreneurs, Journal of Enterprising Communities, Vol. 3 No. 1, 2009 pp. 8-24.

3. Baron, R.A. (2004). The cognitive perspective: A valuable tool for answering entrepreneurship's basic "why" questions. Journal of Business Venturing, 19(2), 221-239.

4. Collins, C.J., P.J. Hanges & E.A. Locke. (2004). The relationship of achievement motivation to entrepreneurial behavior: A meta-analysis. Human Performance, 17, 95–117.

5. Stewart, W.H. & P.L. Roth. (2001). Risk propensity differences between entrepreneurs and managers: A meta-analytic review. Journal of Applied Psychology, 86, 145-153.

6. Zhao, H. & S.E. Seibert. (2006). The big five personality dimensions and entrepreneurial status: A meta-analytical review. Journal of Applied Psychology, 91, 259-271.

7. Goleman D., et. al. (2013). Primal Leadership: Realizing the power of Emotional Intelligence. Cambridge, MA: Harvard Business School Publishing.

8. https://www.tojqi.net/index.php/journal/article/view/4084

9. Zampetakis, L. A., Kafetsios, K., Bouranta, N., Dewett, T. & Moustakis, V.S. (2009). On the relationship between emotional intelligence and entrepreneurial attitudes and intentions. *International Journal of Entrepreneurial Behavior & Research*, *15*, 595-618.

10. https://mashelkar.com/speeches/on-designing-an-indian-agriculture-inclusive-innovation-system/

11. https://nutrifix.co/

12. https://mashelkar.com/speeches/leveraging-agritech-startups-in-indian-agriculture-innovation-ecosystem/

13. https://www.bighaat.com/

14. http://www.flybirdinnovations.com/

15. https://ninjacart.in/

16. https://yourstory.com/2016/07/ravgo/amp

17. https://www.freshglow.co/

18. https://nrf.com/blog/how-one-entrepreneurs-simple-idea-reducing-food-waste

19. https://farmkartgroup.com/from-farmer-to-entrepreneur-the-agripreneur/

Chapter 3 - Creativity: Unleashing Earthworms of Entrepreneurial Innovation

1. Gurteen, D. (1998). Knowledge, creativity and innovation. Journal of Knowledge Management, 2(1), 5-13. doi:10.1108/13673279810800744.

2. Puccio, G., & Grivas, C. (2009). Examining the relationship between personality traits and creativity styles. Creativity and Innovation Management, 18(4), 247-255. doi:10.1111/j.1467-8691.2009.00535.

3. Kabir, M. N. (2019). Innovation. Knowledge-Based Social Entrepreneurship, 163–204. https://doi.org/10.1057/978-1-137-34809-8_6

4. Lane, P. J., Koka, B. R., & Pathak, S. (2006). The Reification of Absorptive Capacity: A Critical Review and Rejuvenation of the Construct. The Academy of Management Review, 31(4), 833–863. https://www.jstor.org/stable/20159255

5. https://blog.plantwise.org/2018/09/06/the-role-of-earthworms-in-sustainable-agriculture/

6. https://krishijagran.com/agriculture-world/farmers-desi-jugaad-to-keep-birds-out-of-crops-impresses-netizens/

7. https://www.responsibletourismindia.com/inspire-me/how-the-indian-jugaad-can-offer-simple-solutions-to-real-life-challenges/552

8. https://www.ecoideaz.com/innovative-green-ideas/jugaad-innovations-indian-farmers

9. Jugaad Innovation Book by Navi Rajdou, Jaydeep Prabhu & Simone Ahuja

10. https://www.manage.gov.in/publications/Success%20Stories%20-%20Farmers%20.pdf

11. 'Psychological Capital: What Lies Beneath.' *Rotman Magazine*, Fall 2008.

12. http://mashelkar.com/articles/more-from-less-for-more-mlm-the-power-of-inclusive-innovation/

13. https://www.gsb.stanford.edu/insights/entrepreneur-finds-scarcity-great-teacher

14. https://thepurposeisprofit.com/2014/04/24/entrepreneurs-scarcity-and-success/

15. https://www.scientificamerican.com/article/distractions-lower-our-iq/

16. https://nif.org.in/Innovationofday/multi-tree-climber-dn-venkat/22

17. https://www.telecomreviewasia.com/news/network-news/3431-jio-announces-campaign-to-replace-india-s-250-million-2g-users#:~:text=Chairman%20of%20Reliance%20Jio%2C%20Mr,cusp%20of%20a%205G%20revolution.%22

18. https://timesofindia.indiatimes.com/gadgets-news/reliance-launches-cheapest-internet-enabled-phone-in-india-jiobharat-phone/articleshow/101461686.cms

19. https://news24online.com/tech/jio-bharat-phone-get-internet-enabled-connectivity-at-just-rs-999-dont-miss-out-psg/147334/

PART 2- GROWTH OF SAPLING = ESTABLISHING A STARTUP

Chapter 4 - The Art of Growth: Lessons from the Bonsai Tree

1. https://bonsairesourcecenter.com/indoor-bonsai-tree-lifespan-how-long-do-bonsai-trees-live/

2. https://www.industryleadersmagazine.com/the-worlds-oldest-how-culture-shaped-japanese-companies/#:~:text=In%20 2019%2C%20there%20were%20over,business%20for%20 over%201000%20years.

3. https://hbr.org/2018/09/how-winning-organizations-last-100-years

4. https://guide.michelin.com/sg/en/article/features/omotenashi

5. https://www.bonsaiempire.com/inspiration/top-10/oldest-bonsai-trees#:~:text=(%231)%20Ficus%20Bonsai%20 tree,Bonsai%20tree%20in%20the%20world.

6. https://www.bbc.com/worklife/article/20200211-why-are-so-many-old-companies-in-japan#:~:text=Back%20in%202008%2C%20a%20Bank,research%20firm%20Teikoku%20Data%20Bank.

7. https://thebeautifultruth.org/world/bonsai-tree-business/

8. https://medium.com/sangfroid-studio/what-can-bonsai-teach-us-about-branding-5e61b9620fe7

9. https://letsgrowleaders.com/2019/07/01/11-inspiring-leadership-secrets-from-bonsai/

10. https://letsgrowleaders.com/2019/07/01/11-inspiring-leadership-secrets-from-bonsai/

Chapter 5 - Vitamin M: Mentorship & Money as Nutrients for Success

1. https://www.plantsnap.com/blog/plant-nutrients/

2. https://hortamericas.com/blog/science/the-importance-of-knowing-basics-of-plant-nutrition/

3. https://extension.wvu.edu/lawn-gardening-pests/news/2021/08/01/how-plants-use-nutrients#:~:text=Nutrients%20are%20essential%20elements%20that,of%20nutrients%20to%20support%20growth.

4. https://ideas.ted.com/the-5-types-of-mentors-you-need-in-your-life

5. http://mashelkar.com/articles/mentoring-view-from-a-personal-lens-11-nov-2017/

6. https://hamdalafertilizer.com/index.php/2020/06/27/fertilizers-are-not-the-same-as-pesticides/

7. https://finmark.com/how-to-find-angel-investors/

Chapter 6 - Weathering the Storm: Building Resilient Startups

1. https://greenupside.com/how-to-protect-your-tomato-plants-from-cold-and-frost/

2. https://mesh4.co.uk/how-to-prevent-wind-damage-on-your-farm-or-rural-property

3. https://www.businessinsider.com/nine-companies-that-destroyed-their-largest-competitors-2011-8?IR=T#blockbuster-vs-netflix-8

4. https://www.livemint.com/news/india/chutta-nahi-hai-how-upi-is-killing-toffee-business-11665720418470.html

5. https://www.heraldgoa.in/Edit/Covid19-gave-a-blow-to-the-candy-industry-too/195193

6. https://blog.proofhub.com/startup-business-is-a-competition-heres-how-you-can-beat-it-bc227df2787

7. https://www.toptal.com/finance/business-model-consultants/competitive-strategy-examples

8. https://www.cbinsights.com/research/report/business-moats-competitive-advantage/

Chapter 7 - Thriving Together: Collaboration Over Competition

1. https://scitechdaily.com/climate-change-and-food-production-affected-by-how-plant-roots-compete-for-underground-real-estate/

2. https://www.frontiersin.org/research-topics/1722/plant-competition-in-a-changing-world

3. https://www.cbinsights.com/research/startup-failure-reasons-top/

4. https://www.forbes.com/sites/forbestechcouncil/2023/05/02/why-it-startups-fail-reasons-trends-and-solutions/?sh=25d5a8053f77

5. https://www.forbes.com/sites/abdoriani/2021/03/18/why-its-ok-to-find-competitors-with-your-startup-idea/?sh=3a16e4b11ed1

6. https://www.luisazhou.com/blog/small-business-statistics/

7. https://www.frontiersin.org/articles/10.3389/fpls.2015.01020/
full#:~:text=Allelopathy%20is%20a%20common%20
biological,detrimental%20effects%20on%20target%20organisms.

8. https://asknature.org/strategy/plant-compounds-protect-from-
competitors/

9. http://www.paulgraham.com/startuplessons.html

10. https://www.forbes.com/sites/abdoriani/2021/03/18/
why-its-ok-to-find-competitors-with-your-startup-
idea/?sh=79cc2ab01ed1

11. https://besjournals.onlinelibrary.wiley.com/doi/10.1111/1365-
2435.12081#:~:text=Plants%20compete%20for%20nutrients%20
by,which%20requires%20maximizing%20root%20length

12. https://scholar.google.com/scholar_lookup?hl=en&publication_
year=1909&author=E.+Warming &title=The+Oecology+of+Plants

13. https://hbr.org/2015/04/a-brief-history-of-the-ways-companies-
compete

14. https://www.qad.com/blog/2017/10/dr-w-edwards-deming-
hero-quality

15. https://journals.plos.org/plosone/article?id=10.1371/journal.
pone.0021114

16. https://www.ncbi.nlm.nih.gov/pmc/articles/
PMC5854654/#:~:text=Legumes%20are%20able%20to%20
form,be%20used%20by%20the%20plant.

17. The collaborative imperative by Ron Ricci and Carl Wiese, https://
www.amazon.com/The-Collaboration-Imperative-RON-RICCI/
dp/098394170X

18. https://www.forbes.com/sites/martinzwilling/2012/05/10/10-
tips-on-the-value-of-collaboration-in-startups/?sh=70f2d8b3e690

19. https://www.almanac.com/content/three-sisters-corn-bean-and-
squash

20. https://www.regent.edu/acad/global/publications/jvl/vol2_
iss1/Grahn_JVLV2I1_p1-5.pdf

21. https://hbr.org/2007/11/eight-ways-to-build-collaborative-teams

22. https://timesofindia.indiatimes.com/gadgets-news/this-is-reliance-jios-first-step-into-metaverse/articleshow/89348426.cms

23. https://www.hindustantimes.com/technology/reliance-announces-tieup-with-these-tech-giants-qualcomm-meta-intel-to-expedite-5g-rollout-in-india-101661765158975.html#:~:text=Jio%20and%20Meta%20are%20collaborating,computing%2C%20and%205G%20edge%20computing.

24. https://www.hindustantimes.com/technology/reliance-announces-tieup-with-these-tech-giants-qualcomm-meta-intel-to-expedite-5g-rollout-in-india-101661765158975.html

25. Rational Exuberance by Michael Mandel (Pg. 38 & 39)

Chapter 8 - Stability & Sustainability: The Cornerstones of a Solid Foundation

1. https://www.amphibio.co/amphigill

2. https://www.biome-renewables.com/powercone

3. https://asknature.org/strategy/tornado-like-spinning-increases-seed-dispersion/

4. http://encyclopedia.uia.org/en/problem/141150

5. https://climatelaunchpad.org/finalists/nanomik-biotechnology/

6. https://asknature.org/innovation/low-cost-portable-toilet-inspired-by-evapotranspiration-in-plants/

7. https://www.globalgoals.org/goals/3-good-health-and-well-being/

8. https://www.who.int/news/item/18-06-2019-1-in-3-people-globally-do-not-have-access-to-safe-drinking-water-unicef-who

9. http://www.change-water.com/

10. https://asknature.org/innovation/low-cost-portable-toilet-inspired-by-evapotranspiration-in-plants/

11. http://www.environmental-expert.com/products/rainmaker-550-solar-distiller-67421

12. https://asknature.org/strategy/seedpod-autorotates/

13. https://www.sycamorefan.com/

14. https://asknature.org/strategy/plant-species-diversity-creates-long-term-stability/

15. https://www.quantumworkplace.com/future-of-work/how-to-create-stability-in-the-workplace

16. https://asknature.org/strategy/spiral-fibers-strengthen-tree-trunk/

17. https://asknature.org/strategy/branching-design-lessens-breakage/

Chapter 9 - Pesticides & Patents: Safeguarding Growth

1. https://pesticidefacts.org/topics/necessity-of-pesticides/#:~:text=Without%20crop%20protection%2C%20including%20pesticides,to%20insects%2C%20diseases%20and%20weeds.&text=Pesticides%20are%20important.,as%20raising%20productivity%20per%20hectare

2. https://www.sciencedirect.com/topics/agricultural-and-biological-sciences/crop-destruction

3. https://www.oecd-ilibrary.org/agriculture-and-food/oecd-fao-agricultural-outlook-2012_agr_outlook-2012-en

4. http://croplifefoundation.files.wordpress.com/2012/07/completed-fungicide-report.pdf

5. https://fruitgrowers.com/the-benefits-of-pesticide-use-in-agriculture/

6. https://bexar-tx.tamu.edu/homehort/archives-of-weekly-articles-davids-plant-of-the-week/natural-defenses-help-make-plants-pest-resistant/

7. https://www.researchgate.net/publication/229524554_An_example_of_varietal_resistance_of_Brussels_sprouts

8. https://asknature.org/strategy/roots-recruit-symbiotic-soil-bacteria/

9. https://www.upcounsel.com/intellectual-property-startup

10. https://www.investindia.gov.in/indian-unicorn-landscape#:~:text=Startup%20Ecosystem%20in%20India,as%20of%2003rd%20October%202023

11. https://www.lexology.com/library/detail.aspx?g=b93536ed-efcc-4ac0-9af1-e9934f8f1b86

Chapter 10 - Insight & Foresight: The Secrets of Plants' Stimulatory Responses

1. https://asknature.org/strategy/leaves-fold-in-response-to-touch/

2. https://www.accenture.com/nl-en/blogs/insights/data-veracity-and-the-future-of-the-digital-economy

3. https://hbr.org/2012/05/empathy-the-most-valuable-thing-they-t

4. https://www.laserfiche.com/ecmblog/why-empathy-is-the-most-important-business-skill/

5. https://www.cnbc.com/2016/10/04/zappos-ceo-tony-hsieh-reveals-3-personality-traits-successful-entrepreneurs-have.html

6. https://asknature.org/strategy/seeds-survive-various-conditions/

7. https://asknature.org/strategy/cells-recognize-and-respond-to-pathogens/

8. Raven, Peter H., and George B. Johnson. "How Plants Grow in Response to Their Environment." Biology. Boston: McGraw-Hill, 2002. 834-35. ; "An Overview of Plant Defenses against Pathogens and Herbivores." Overview of Plant Defenses. N.p., n.d. Web. 16 Sept. 2012.

9. Forterre, Y., Skotheim, J., Dumais, J. *et al.* How the Venus flytrap snaps. *Nature* 433, 421–425 (2005). https://doi.org/10.1038/nature03185

10. https://asknature.org/strategy/stretched-leaves-power-rapid-closure/

11. https://www.inc.com/emily-canal/the-snapbar-pivot-keep-your-city-smiling-coronavirus-pandemic.html

12. https://www.embroker.com/blog/business-uncertainty/

13. https://asknature.org/strategy/flowers-follow-sun/

14. https://www.cilgghana.org/impact-of-leadership-role-on-organizations-performance/#:~:text=Their%20leadership%20motivates%20the%20people,crucial%20component%20of%20effective%20management

PART 3- SEED TO TREE = IDEAS TO IMPACT

Chapter 11 - Synergy: Converging Parallels between Plant Anatomy and Business Units

1. https://ncert.nic.in/textbook/pdf/kebo106.pdf

2. https://extension.missouri.edu/publications/mg2

3. https://courses.lumenlearning.com/wm-introductiontobusiness/chapter/reading-functional-areas-of-business/

4. https://www.superbusinessmanager.com/four-business-functions-in-details/

5. https://blog.zipboard.co/7-reasons-why-teamwork-is-critical-for-your-startup-s-success-d344a386fa92

Chapter 12 - Venturing Boldly: Embracing Risks, Reaping Rewards

1. https://www.fao.org/uploads/media/3-ManagingRiskInternLores.pdf

2. Poppendieck, Mary, and Michael A. Cusumano. "Lean software development: A tutorial." IEEE software 29, no. 5 (2012): 26-32.

3. Bicheno, John, and Matthias Holweg. The lean toolbox. Vol. 4. Buckingham: PICSIE books, 2000.

4. Medium. (2017). How Uber, Airbnb & Dropbox Released MVPs to Achieve Rapid Growth. [online] Available at: https://medium.com/@LoganTjm/how-uber-airbnbdropbox-released-mvps-to-achieve-rapid-growthd823ac6eaed5

5. Muckersie, E. (2017). FreshMinds - 3 examples of lean startup in action. [online] Freshminds.net. Available at: http://www.freshminds.net/2016/09/3-examples-of-leanstartup/

6. Ford, M. and Ford, M. (2017). The Lean Startup Methodology. [online] MATTYFORD. Available at: https://mattyford.com/blog/2014/11/11/the-lean-startupmethodology

7. https://ia801206.us.archive.org/31/items/TheLeanStartupErickRies/The%20Lean%20Startup%20-%20Erick%20Ries.pdf

8. https://www.treehugger.com/plants-can-make-eerily-good-decisions-4866028

9. https://www.cell.com/current-biology/fulltext/S0960-9822%2816%2930459-6

Chapter 13 - Seasonal Adaptations: Navigating Market Shifts

1. https://www.happysprout.com/inspiration/seasons-plants/

2. https://earthsky.org/earth/how-plants-manage-season-shift-from-winter-to-spring/

3. https://www.bl.uk/business-and-ip-centre/articles/how-to-identify-market-trends-for-long-term-business-planning

4. https://theconversation.com/climate-change-is-altering-the-seasonal-rhythm-of-plant-life-cycle-events-181231

5. https://www.napervilleparks.org/learnaboutnature/how-do-plants-survive-winter

6. https://startuptalky.com/kodak-bankruptcy-case-study/#:~:text=The%20ignorance%20of%20new%20

technology%20and%20not%20adapting%20to%20 changing,the%20sales%20of%20digital%20cameras.

7. https://www.cnet.com/tech/computing/history-of-digital-cameras-from-70s-prototypes-to-iphone-and-galaxys-everyday-wonders/#:~:text=The%20first%20digital%20 camera&text=The%20first%20actual%20digital%20 still,invented%20Fairchild%20CCD%20electronic%20sensors.

8. https://brand-minds.medium.com/why-did-kodak-fail-and-what-can-you-learn-from-its-failure-70b92793493c#:~:text=Complacency,%2C%20the%20 roll%2Dfilm%20business

9. https://www.nature.com/articles/s41477-022-01139-5

10. https://www.futurity.org/extremophytes-plants-harsh-conditions-2735182/#:~:text=Extreme%20plants%20speed%20 growing&text=When%20plants%20encounter%20dry%2C%20 salty,the%20plant%20how%20to%20respond

11. https://www.theceomagazine.com/business/innovation-technology/business-boom-pandemic/

12. https://www.mckinsey.com/featured-insights/future-of-work/ from-surviving-to-thriving-reimagining-the-post-covid-19-return

13. https://www.gardeningknowhow.com/garden-how-to/info/ how-plants-survive-extreme-environments.htm#:~:text=High%20 winds%20and%20cold%20temperatures,wind%2C%20 snow%2C%20and%20cold.

14. https://study.com/academy/lesson/how-changes-in-consumer-tastes-affect-business-activity.html

15. Arpita Khare(2011), Impact of Indian Cultural Values and Lifestyles on Meaning of Branded Products: Study on University Students in India, Journal Of International Consumer Marketing,23,5.

16. https://www.ripublication.com/gjmbs_spl/gjmbsv3n8_06.pdf

Chapter 14 - Startups & Rainforests: Embracing Effectiveness for Success

1. https://www.betterup.com/blog/efficiency-vs-effectiveness#:~:text=your%20team%20goals.-,Efficiency%20versus%20effectiveness%20defined,or%20achieves%20a%20better%20outcome.

2. https://qz.com/1061207/atacama-desert-the-driest-place-on-earth-is-blooming-with-flowers-after-surprise-rainfall/

3. Victor Hwang and Greg Horowitt, through their book *"The Rainforest: The Secret to Building the Next Silicon Valley*, Regenwald, 2012.

4. https://www.abc.net.au/news/health/2016-05-12/edible-weeds-and-how-you-can-use-them/7406004#:~:text=Dandelion%20is%20probably%20one%20of, cooked%20and%20eaten%20like%20spinach.

5. https://www.technologyreview.com/1997/11/01/102239/what-i-learned-in-the-rainforest/

6. https://www.futurity.org/tropical-forests-diversity-1895542/

7. https://www.open.edu/openlearn/nature-environment/environmental-studies/undestanding-the-environment-flows-and-feedback/content-section-2.4

8. R. Gopalakrishnan, Sushmita Srivastava through their book "How Kiran Mazumdar Shaw fermented Biocon," 2020

9. https://www.weforum.org/agenda/2021/11/why-diversity-within-your-organization-matters/#:~:text=The%20more%20a%20organization%20is,enhances%20deliberation%20and%20upends%20conformity

10. https://hinounou.com/

11. http://mashelkar.com/speeches/integration-innovation-inclusion-pathways-to-progress/

12. https://asknature.org/innovation/paint-inspired-by-lotus-leaves-creates-self-cleaning-and-antifouling-surfaces/

13. https://stemazing.org/wp-content/uploads/2017/07/lotusPaint.pdf

14. https://inhabitat.com/researchers-develop-plant-inspired-structures-that-can-move/

15. https://thespaces.com/biomimicry-explore-buildings-that-are-shaped-like-trees/

16. Sarbalé ke sculptural installation by Francis Kéré at Coachella. Photography: Lance Gerber, courtesy of Coachella

Chapter 15 - Incentivizing Innovation: The Bee-Nectar Way

1. http://www.anneleonard.com/nutritional-ecology-of-floral-rewards

2. https://www.thesuccessfactory.co.uk/blog/11-ideas-for-rewarding-innovation-in-the-workplace

3. Prasifka J.R et al., Using nectar-related traits to enhance crop-pollinator interactions. Frontiers in Plant Science, 2018. 9: 1–8.

4. Yan J. et al., Pollinator responses to floral colour change, nectar, and scent promote reproductive fitness in Quisqualis indica (Combretaceae). Scientific Reports, 2016. 6: 1–10.

5. Petanidou T. and Lamborn E., A land for flowers and bees: Studying pollination ecology in Mediterranean communities. Plant Biosystems – An International Journal Dealing with All Aspects of Plant Biology, 2005. 139: 279–294.

6. Woodcock T.S. et al., Flies and flowers II: Floral attractants and rewards. Journal of Pollination Ecology, 2014. 12: 63–94.

7. Ghosh S. et al., Pollination mechanisms and adaptations in flower and ornamental crops- A review. Journal of Pharmacognosy & Phytochemistry, 2017. 6:662–665.

READER'S NOTES